NOW *THAT'S* A LINZERTORTE!

Revised 2nd Edition - 2006

30 Years of Recipes and Vermont Stories

from

The Trapp Family Lodge

By: Marshall Faye
Executive Pastry Chef

Edited by: R. Pierce Reid

[signature: Marshall R. Faye]

Acknowledgements:
All recipes in this book are made using King Arthur Flour
Family photos submitted by Marshall Faye
Mt. Washington photo courtesy Louise Ebbett Tipton
Cover design, diagrams and digital photos by Lindsay Total Graphics

© 2003; 2006 - Book Layout, Design, and Production by:
LINDSAY TOTAL GRAPHICS
and its licensors.
Manchester, Connecticut

Table of Contents

Introduction: The Most Unlikely Pastry Chef In The World ...   6
Author's Note   8
Life In The Kingdom...   9

Recipes

Section 1 – Breads..   11
Crusty Country Loaf..   12
Early American Open Hearth Bread   13
Spicy Batter Bread   15
Sweet Dream Bread   16
Fougasse Loaf   17
Fresh Onion Bread   19
Healthy Oat Bran Bread   20
Hearty Peasant Bread   21
Bacon and Walnut Bread   23
Bonnie's Banana Bread   24
Zesty Herb Bread..   25
Sour Cherry Rye   27
Walnut Bread   28
Herb Flat Bread For Dipping   29
Tuscan Style Rosemary & Raisin Bread............................   31
Breakfast On The Go Bread   32
Kaiser Bread   33
Light Rye Bread   37
Mediterranean Bread   39
Mushroom Bread   41
Pain au Chocolate *(Chocolate Bread)*   42
Pain du Champagne *(French Country Bread)*...................   43
Ciabatta Bread...   45
Soft Wheat Dinner Rolls...   47
Sweet Oatmeal Bread (As Featured In *Gourmet* Magazine) ...   49
Vienna Braided Bread   51

ISBN 0-9747872-0-5

Recipes – Continued

Section 2 – Pies, Cakes, and Tarts 53

Alpen Apfel Cake *(Mountain Apple Cake)* 55
Island Coconut Custard Pie 57
Crustless Apfel Pie 59
Apricot and Almond Tart 61
Mohn Torte *(Christmas Cake)* 62
Hungarian Cheesecake 63
Lemon Chess Pie 65
Whole Wheat Maple Apple Tart 67
Tart and Tangy Key Lime Pie 69
Marshall's Vermont Maple Cream Pie 70
Vermont Maple Walnut Cake 71

Section 3 – Tortes 73

Marshall's World Famous Linzertorte 75
Lemon Frangipan Torte 78
Nut Streusel Sour Cream Torte 81
Poppy Seed Torte 83
Sachertorte *(Sugar Torte)* 85
Salzberg Lemon Torte 87
Winter Apricot Torte 89

Section 4 – Desserts 91

Austrian Apfel Strudel 93
Fresh Fruit Flan 95
Trapp Family Babka 97

Section 5 – Cookies and Crackers 99

Almond Cookies 101
Orange Bisquits 103
Cranberry White Chocolate Chip Cookies 104
Mandel Makronen *(Almond Macaroons)* 105
Amandel Fierkken *(Almond Streusel Squares)* 107
Hazelnuss Pfeffernuse 109
Old Towne Molasses Cookies 110
Chocolate Crackle Cookies 111

Recipes – Continued

Fruit Pinwheels 112

Good Ol' Gingersnaps 113

Murbe Haselnuss Stargerl *(Short Dough Hazelnut Bars)* 115

Ischeler Krapferln 116

Lemon Rings 117

Butternut Cookies 119

Poppy Cheese Sticks 120

Mt. Mansfield Maple Pecan Drop Cookies 121

Othello Cookies 122

Pecan Snowballs 123

Country Sunshine Crackers 125

Corn and Cheddar Crackers 126

Rugalah 127

Spitzbuben Cookies *(Rascals)* 128

Super Shortbread Cookies 129

Chocolate Pecan Crescents 131

Chocolate Apricot Chews 132

Topfen Kipferl *(Cheese Croissants)* 133

Vermont Cheddar Cheese Crackers 134

Cranberry Almond Delights 135

Rum Walnuss Horns 137

Section 6 – Breakfast Treats **139**

Hot Homemade English Muffins 140

Citrus Buns 141

Cheddar and Pepper Scones 142

Lowfat Deer Camp Doughnuts 143

St. Timothy's Coffee Cake 145

Sticky Wheat Breakfast Buns 146

Stowe's Finest Maple Oatmeal Muffins 147

Section 7 – Confections **149**

Dark Chocolate Pecan Truffles 150

Reader's Notes **151**

Stories

Life In The Northeast Kingdom 9
Growing Up In The Kingdom 14
The Victory-Granby Bog 18
The Gray Ghost 22
The Fire Will Be There When We Get There 26
Fill 'er Up Mister? 30
Camp: A Vermont Tradition 34
I Can Get Turned Around In My Back Yard 36
Coming Of Age In Vermont 38
Scared Straight 40
"I'll Give You $200 A Month More" 44
Short Stories From The Bakery 46
Life In The CIA 48
Two Chefs For The Price Of One 50
"I Gotta Meet This Girl" 54
Giving Them Something To Listen To 56
Poker Winnings 58
Not Only My Wife, But My Best Friend 60
Stowe, Vermont In The '70s. 64
All Our Pets Were Edible 66
Happy To Be Picked Second 68
"Now *That's* A Linzertorte!" 74
Our Mailorder House 76
You Must Be My Most Reliable Employee 80
The Things We Do For Our Guests 82
Workin' In A Coal Mine 84
Maria's Sweet Tooth 86
The Ghost Of Trapp Hill Road 88
Praying For A Cuppa 92
We Were All Part Of The von Trapp Family 94
What Goes "WOOF!" And Eats Apples? 96
The Most Horrible Night That Anyone Can Remember 100
Raising 46 Children 102
Professor Marshall 106
Moscow, Vermont Style 108
"Dad, I Want To Be A Chef" 114
A Few Fish Stories 118
My Daughter The Athlete 124
My Fifteen Minutes 130
The Saga Of Big Ben 136
Prayer Answered Or Amazing Coincidence 144

The Most Unlikely Pastry Chef
In the World

If you ask most Americans to define a Yankee, they will tell you that it's a person from the Northeast. Ask a Northeasterner to define a Yankee and he will tell you it's a person from New England. Ask a New Englander to define a Yankee and he will tell you it's a person from Vermont. Ask a Vermonter to define a Yankee and he will tell you it's a person from St. Johnsbury. And ask a St. Johnsbury native to define a Yankee and he will tell you it's a person who eats pie for breakfast.

By any definition Marshall Faye is a Yankee. Marshall Faye is also the last person on earth who you would expect to be a world-class pastry chef.

If you met him on the street or – more likely – in the woods, you would think Marshall is a lumberjack, a truck driver or a north woods fishing guide. And when he engulfs you in a bear hug and lets loose with his textbook Vermont Yankee accent, you wonder how this ninth-generation Vermonter and son of an Abenaki Indian became a baker and pastry chef of world-wide renown.

Yet he did.

Marshall built his reputation in a place that is synonymous with fine food and particularly fine pastries – the Trapp Family Lodge in Stowe, Vermont. Tens of thousands of guests flock each year to this Stowe landmark. And for most visitors, the trip would not be complete without indulging in some of the finest tortes, cakes, and confections outside of Vienna, Austria.

Not only has Marshall filled the pastry carts and bread baskets at von Trapp's for years, his recipes have also been featured in several regional cookbooks and in publications such as *Gourmet Magazine, Bon Appetite, Saveur, and Country Journal*. And his Linzertortes were featured on a major home shopping TV network which sold thousands of tortes in a matter of minutes.

But it is the time Marshall has spent with the guests at the lodge that have given him the most professional satisfaction – and the impetus to write his book. Over the years he has given cooking lessons to hundreds of von Trapp Family Lodge and timeshare guests who have not only learned baking and pastry recipes... but who have listened with rapt attention as Marshall combined baking tips with his stories of growing up and living in Vermont.

In the pages of this, his first cookbook, Marshall shares some of his favorite recipes and he shares stories of Vermont; his passion for the outdoors; his family; and his 30 years working with – and being friends with – the von Trapp Family.

So enjoy the recipes and indulge in some fun and easy pastry cooking at home. But also take some time to relax and enjoy stories as only a real Yankee can tell them. And enjoy a few glimpses of Vermont as it was... as it is... and as it probably always will be.

Author's Note

I've had the privilege of working at the Trapp Family Lodge as the baker, bakery manager and executive pastry chef for the past 30 years, starting not long before the tragic fire that destroyed the lodge in 1980.

From the ashes, a new and better lodge has arisen and it continues to grow and offer not only wonderful food and hospitality, but a place that has brought me close to hundreds of guests who have taken cooking classes and learned their way around a bakery.

I started teaching classes after regular hours for our timeshare and lodge guests. My first classes were held not long after the fire when we were looking for all kinds of new ways to keep people coming to the hotel. At the time not many professional chefs were offering baking classes to the public and these classes proved a big hit. And it has always been my pleasure to show people how easy it is to bake.

While I was teaching, I got into the habit of entertaining our guests with stories about my life, family and friends. Soon the stories about growing up in Vermont – and about my 30 years at the lodge – became as much a part of the class as the recipes and the kitchen technique. People came back year after year not only to learn, but to be entertained.

Doing something fun together, sharing parts of each other's lives and taking away a sense of accomplishment – that tastes good – became the basis for my cooking classes.

Every year my students and guests would ask me: "When are you going to write a book, Marshall?"

Well, thanks to their dogged persistence and to my young friend Pierce Reid who helped me put the words and commas together, this book of recipes and stories was born.

Pierce Reid and I visualized this book as one that would give our readers easy and immediate access to the time needed for preparation prior to baking, the utensils needed, as well as the more classic cookbook components. And as we did so, I could think of no one else who would be more naturally fit to render this book for printing than the person who shared many of my early memories, my lifelong friend, Guy Lindsay.

And now, here it is. My first cookbook.

Enjoy!

Life In The Northeast Kingdom

The Northeast Kingdom of Vermont, where I grew up, is the part of Vermont to the east and north of St. Johnsbury. It is bordered by Canada to the north and the Connecticut river to the east. Towns like Danville, Walden, Granby and Maidstone are all part of the Kingdom with St. Johnsbury serving as the hub of the region. The Kingdom is by far the wildest and least developed part of Vermont and much of its woods and northern swampland have never been farmed or developed so they are just as they were hundreds of years ago. It is truly the "big woods."

The Kingdom got its name because at one point that region was going to secede from the United States and form its own nation. The people there were – and are – so fiercely independent that they didn't want anyone telling them what to do.

St. Johnsbury used to be a thriving town and a center of commerce. For industry there was dairy processing, machine tool and precision manufacturing, woodworking and furniture making, and of course maple syrup and sugar. There is still some beautiful architecture and St. Johnsbury has a fantastically-preserved Victorian downtown.

These days the whole Kingdom is pretty economically depressed. But the people in the Northeast Kingdom will survive no matter what. Whatever the economy of the country is like, people will get by because they know how to grow their own gardens, smoke their own meat, and preserve their own vegetables. People in the Northeast Kingdom are as self-sufficient today as the frontier settlers of a hundred years ago.

You won't find the hustle and bustle of Boston or New York – or even Burlington. But you will find people who can always do a lot when all they have is a little.

A lot of people think Vermonters – especially Vermonters from the Northeast Kingdom – are pretty quiet and taciturn. They think that we aren't very outgoing. And that's not true. We are very friendly and warm to anyone who comes up our way.

Unless you tell us what to do or how to do it. And then you're going to get in trouble!

Breads

Crusty Country Loaf

Ingredients:

8 ¼ cups all-purpose flour

¾ cup dark rye flour

1 Tbsp. and 1 tsp. salt.

3 Tbsp. Saf-instant yeast

3 ½ cups warm water *(about 110 degrees)*

¼ cup sourdough starter
   (see Pain du Champagne Page 35)

1 egg white, beaten, for brushing on loaves

½ cup yellow cornmeal for sprinkling on baking pan

Utensils:

Large bowl

Floured board

Lightly oiled baking
   sheet

Preparation time: 45 minutes

Oven temp: 375°F

Baking time: About 25 - 35 minutes

Results: 2 large loaves

Instructions:

1. Place all ingredients, except egg and corn meal, in a large bowl, with water going in last.

2. Mix into straight dough and turn out dough onto floured board.

3. Knead for 8 minutes. Cover and put in a warm place to rise for 10 minutes.

4. Re-knead to knock back rise and form dough into two oval loaves.

5. Place on baking sheet that has been sprinkled with corn meal, brush with egg and dust with white flour.

6. Allow to rise until loaves double in size. Preheat oven to 375°F and bake loaves for 25 - 35 minutes until golden and crusty. Serve warm; slice at the table.

Early American Open Hearth Bread

Ingredients:
7 cups unbleached flour
½ cup millet meal or bran
½ cup black strap molasses
4 whole eggs
2 Tbsp. Saf-instant yeast
1 Tbsp. Vermont honey
2 cups warm *(110 degrees)* milk
¼ cup bear fat
   (vegetable oil is an acceptable substitute outside of Vermont)
3 tsp. sea salt (or table salt)
1 cup yellow cornmeal for sprinkling on loaves
2 Tbsp. melted butter for brushing on loaves

Utensils:
Large bowl
Floured board
Two well-greased
  bread pans

Preparation time: 30 minutes
Oven temp: 375°F
Baking time: About 45 - 60 minutes
Results: 2 large loaves

Instructions:
1. Place eggs in bowl and beat lightly.
2. Add all remaining ingredients, putting in milk last.
3. Mix into straight dough and turn out dough onto floured board.
4. Knead lightly for 2 minutes. Cover and put in a warm place to rise until loaves double.
5. Re-knead to knock back rise and form dough into two round loaves.
6. Place in well-greased bread pans. Brush with melted butter and sprinkle with yellow corn meal.
7. Allow to rise to top of baking pans.
8. Preheat oven to 375°F and bake loaves for 45 - 60 minutes until golden and crusty. Slice when hot.

Growing Up In The Kingdom

I grew up in the Northeast Kingdom in the 1950s and it was a lot more Norman Rockwell than *Happy Days*.

Northern Vermont in the '50s was the perfect place to grow up – paradise for a kid. I played Little League baseball and became a Life Scout. Like most kids, I hunted and fished from the time I was old enough to walk. There was a river right outside my house that was full of trout.

Summers were fantastic. The weather was cool and crisp and clear. There were berries growing wild all around the area and you could drink out of any stream. My friends and I would go out camping and we would shoot our .22s. There were rivers to swim in, ponds to fish and woods to explore – all right out the back door. Every day was an adventure.

I went to school at the St. Johnsbury Academy and, of course, we walked to school every day. There were a couple of busses for the kids who lived way out in the country, but lots of kids had a couple of miles to walk. And for anyone who has ever been through a winter in St. J., that is hard work. I don't remember that we ever had a snow day. But they did close school during mud season when the roads turned into mud a foot deep and you couldn't get anywhere.

Mud season is still a Vermont tradition.

Often in the fall, we would get up early before school to go hunting. Showing up at school with your deer rifle was an everyday thing during the fall. Lots of kids took off school during deer season. Partly for fun, but mainly because a lot of families needed every deer or bear or rabbit or partridge they could get. That was food on the table for the coming winter and the kids had to hunt along with the rest of the men in the family. In some parts of the Kingdom that's still true today.

Though these days, hunting is a right of passage for many girls as well.

Spicy Batter Bread

Ingredients:

5 cups all-purpose flour

2 tsp. salt

2 tsp. soft butter

1 ½ Tbsp. Saf-instant yeast

3 cups warm water *(about 110 degrees F)*

¼ tsp. nutmeg

¼ tsp. mace

⅛ tsp. ginger

⅛ tsp. clove

1 cup plumped raisins

Utensils:

Large bowl

Two greased and
    floured bread pans

Preparation time: 45 minutes

Oven temp: 350°F

Baking time: 30 - 45 minutes

Results: 2 loaves

Instructions:

1. **Place all ingredients except water in bowl, without mixing.**

2. **Add water and mix to smooth batter – cover with clean wrap and let rise to double in size in warm place.**

3. **Mix lightly with spoon – pour into gresed and floured pans.**

4. **Dust lightly with flour and rise again to top of pans.**

5. **Bake at 350°F for 30 - 45 minutes.**

Sweet Dream Bread

Ingredients:

3 cups warm milk

$\frac{1}{2}$ cup butter *(1 stick)*

2 tsp. salt

$\frac{1}{4}$ cup light brown sugar

$\frac{1}{4}$ tsp. mace

1 whole egg

2 Tbsp. grated orange rind

2 Tbsp. grated lemon rind

2 Tbsp. Saf-instant yeast

6 cups unbleached all-purpose flour

1 cup mixed raisins *(or any other dried fruit)*

1 cup sliced almonds

Utensils:
Large bowl
Cookie sheet

Preparation time: 25 minutes
Oven temp: 350°F
Baking time: 25 minutes
Results: 4 small loaves

Instructions:

1. **Place all ingredients in mixing bowl and stir together. When the dough is mixed, knead it for about 8 minutes, then allow it to rest.**

2. **Divide dough in 4 loaf sized pieces and form each piece into an oval shape. Fold the oval over once and brush with beaten egg.**

3. **Allow the dough to rise until doubled in size and bake at 350°F for approximately 25 minutes.**

4. **When cool, brush the loaves with melted butter and roll them in white granulated sugar.**

Ingredients:

4 cups all-purpose flour
2 cups warm water *(about 110 degrees)*
$\frac{1}{8}$ cup olive oil
1 $\frac{1}{2}$ tsp. fresh, chopped or powdered rosemary
1 $\frac{1}{2}$ Tbsp. Saf-instant yeast
$\frac{1}{2}$ cup grated parmesan cheese
1 $\frac{1}{2}$ tsp. thyme
1 $\frac{1}{2}$ tsp. basil
1 tsp. fresh garlic, chopped
1 Tbsp. salt
1 Tbsp. coarse salt or sea salt for sprinkling on loaves

Utensils:

Large bowl
Floured board
Baking sheet, lightly
  brushed with olive oil
Sharp knife

Preparation time: 35 minutes

Oven temp: 425°F
Baking time: About 20 - 25 minutes
Results: 4 loaves

Instructions:

1. **Place all ingredients except coarse salt in a bowl, adding water last.**

2. **Mix to a straight dough and turn out dough onto floured board.**

3. **Knead for 8 minutes. Cover and put in a warm place to rise for 20 minutes.**

4. **Divide in half and flatten each piece into a rectangle about $\frac{1}{2}$ inch thick and twice as long as wide. Cut 4 slits in each piece and stretch apart slightly so it looks like a ladder.**

5. **Place on baking sheet that has been lightly brushed with olive oil. Brush loaves with olive oil and sprinkle with coarse salt and grated parmesan cheese.**

6. **Preheat oven to 425°F and bake loaves for 20 - 25 minutes until crust is golden and crisp. Serve with hummus, tearing off pieces to dip.**

The Victory-Granby Bog

A friend of mine when I was growing up was a gentleman named Fred Mould. Fred was the curator of the Fairbanks Museum in St. Johnsbury. He was also one of the first naturalists to be instrumental in preserving a large piece of Vermont land. That piece of land was the Victory-Granby bog.

The Victory-Granby bog is one of the major features of the Northeast Kingdom and it is really unlike any other area in New England. The area is several thousand acres that are almost completely undisturbed and quite pristine. Today, there are some marked paths through sections of the bog and it is a wonderful nature preserve for people who really want to see how wild Vermont can be. You have to see it to believe it.

But when I was growing up, it was completely unmarked. And also dangerous if you were not careful. Even today, few people venture any distance into the bog.

The only time I went into it, I was with an older friend. Very quickly we got lost and before long it was pitch dark. We thrashed around for a while and finally got onto a dry spot. Luckily, I leaned against a tree to rest and the tree was humming! I pointed this out to my friend who realized where we were. The "tree" was actually a utility pole and we were able to follow the power line to the road.

As an aside, Fred Mould was the person who convinced me that it was ok to be a chef. Back when I was thinking about going to cooking school, a lot of my friends told me that cooking was women's work and that I shouldn't pursue a career as a chef. Not a very politically-correct attitude, even in the '60s. But Fred said that it was all right to do what I wanted to do. His opinion really mattered to me and I wanted to be a chef, so that was that.

Today, in Granby, there is a beautiful big boulder with a plaque on it recognizing Fred for his work.

That's how Vermont's first naturalist helped me to become a pastry chef!

Fresh Onion Bread

Ingredients:

4 cups all-purpose flour
$\frac{1}{2}$ Tbsp. salt
1 whole egg
1 Tbsp. granulated sugar
1 Tbsp. olive oil
1 $\frac{1}{2}$ Tbsp. Saf-instant yeast
1 $\frac{1}{2}$ cups warm water *(about 90 – 100 degrees)*
Poppy seeds
2 cups fresh onion, chopped fine
$\frac{1}{2}$ tsp. bakers color *(if desired)*
$\frac{1}{2}$ cup yellow cornmeal to sprinkle on pan
1 egg, beaten

Utensils:

Large bowl
Floured board
Baking sheet sprinkled
  with cornmeal
Sharp knife

Preparation time: 30 minutes

Oven temp: 400°F

Baking time. About 25 minutes or
  until golden

Results: 2 loaves

Instructions:

1. Mix the flour, sugar, oil, egg, salt, yeast, baker's color, and onion into a straight dough, adding the water last.
2. Turn onto a floured board and knead for 10 minutes, adding a small amount of water if necessary.
3. Allow dough to rest for 10 minutes, then divide into two halves and shape into round loaves.
4. Flatten dough slightly on baking sheet that has been sprinkled with corn meal.
5. Lightly brush with beaten egg and sprinkle with poppy seeds.
6. Put loaves into a warm place and allow them to rise until they double in size.
7. Preheat oven to 400°F. Bake for about 25 minutes or until golden. When fully baked, the loaves will have a hollow sound when tapped. Serve warm.

Healthy Oat Bran Bread*

Ingredients:
6 cups high gluten flour
2 ½ cups warm water *(about 110 degrees)*
½ cup wheat bran
½ cup oat bran
¾ cup rolled oats *(not instant or minute)*
½ cup brown sugar, tightly packed
⅛ cup canola oil
½ tsp. cider vinegar
1 ½ Tbsp. Saf-instant yeast
1 cup rolled oats *(not instant or minute)* to sprinkle on top
White from one small egg, beaten

Utensils:
Large bowl
Floured board
Baking sheet lightly
  brushed with canola oil
Sharp knife

Preparation time: 30 minutes
Oven temp: 375°F
Baking time: 45 - 60 minutes until
  golden
Results: 2 loaves

Instructions:
1. **Place oil, brown sugar, and vinegar into 110 degree water.**
2. **Add oat bran, wheat bran, ¾ cup rolled oats, and flour, adding yeast last.**
3. **Work into a smooth dough and turn onto floured board.**
4. **Knead 10 minutes and allow to rest for 20 minutes.**
5. **Form into two loaves.**
6. **Brush with egg white and roll in the oats reserved for sprinkling on top.**
7. **Slice top of bread and place on baking pan.**
8. **Set in a warm place until loaves double in size.**
9. **Preheat oven to 375°F and bake for 45 - 60 minutes until golden. When baked, the loaves will sound hollow when tapped. Serve warm.**

* indicates a healthy choice recipe – no salt, no cholesterol

Hearty Peasant Bread

Ingredients:

2 ¾ cups warm water
4 cups all-purpose flour
2 cups dark rye flour
¼ cup rye chops
2 Tbsp. Saf-instant yeast
1 Tbsp. salt
1 Tbsp. molasses
1 Tbsp. vegetable oil
½ cup chopped cooked bacon
1 cup shredded sharp Vermont Cheddar or
  Emmentaler Swiss cheese
¼ cup chopped yellow onion
¼ cup yellow corn meal sprinkled on baking pan
1 egg white, beaten, to brush on loaves

Utensils:

Large bowl
Floured board
Baking sheet lightly oiled
Sharp knife

Preparation time: 30 minutes
Oven temp: 400°F
Baking time: About 25 - 35 minutes
Results: 2 loaves

Instructions:

1. Place all ingredients, except the egg white, into a large bowl, adding water last.
2. Mix together into a straight dough and turn onto floured board.
3. Knead 8 minutes and allow to rest for 10 to 15 minutes.
4. Form into two doughnut-shaped loaves, using thumbs to put a hole in the middle.
5. Brush with egg white and sprinkle with dark rye flour or all-purpose flour.
6. Slice top of bread and place on baking pan.
7. Set in a warm place until loaves double in size.
8. Preheat oven to 400°F and bake for 25 - 35 minutes until browned. When baked, the loaves will sound hollow when tapped. Serve warm or cool.

The Gray Ghost

Vermont Yankees have a reputation for being pretty frugal. Because we often didn't have much, we learned to squeeze the last bit of value out of things. Johannes von Trapp once even called me a parsimonious Vermonter. The Gray Ghost is a lesson in Yankee frugality at its finest.

In 1960 a new truck appeared in my father's driveway. Christened "The Gray Ghost" it was a Willys pickup truck and it was the latest thing in four-wheel drive! In those days, there were very few four-wheel-drive trucks in Vermont – or anywhere. These days, everyone has sport utility vehicles. But to be driving a Willys pickup in 1960 in St. Johnsbury... that made my dad's snow plowing operation a cutting-edge business!

My dad had that truck for all the years he was at the garage. I even learned to drive in it. Later on, I bought the Gray Ghost from him. By then it had 175,000 miles on it but it was just beginning its second life! I took it back and forth to work and to deer camp, drove it all over New England, hauled firewood out of the woods, and even took it up into Northern Canada. And when my kids got big

enough to reach the pedals, they had their first driving lessons in it.

By the time it had 300,000 miles on it, I was having trouble scrounging for parts and had welded the frame several times. Finally, I couldn't get it inspected any more because it was too rusty. So I put it beside the road with a 'for sale' sign on it. I was asking $400, but if anyone had offered $100, I'd have gladly let them take it away! I couldn't believe it when someone showed up and paid the whole $400! But he was happy to get it and he rebuilt it and he went on to drive it for years.

Last I knew, The Gray Ghost had gone to a junkyard in Wolcott, Vermont. But it still wasn't ready for the scrap heap! Despite its 400,000 miles, the junkyard owner loaded it up with welding equipment and still uses it as a service truck and a yard donkey.

The Gray Ghost was a true Vermonter. It worked forever and didn't know the meaning of the word "quit."

Bacon and Walnut Bread

Ingredients:

1 Tbsp. olive oil

½ cup bacon, cooked and chopped

¾ cup walnut pieces

4 ½ cups unbleached all-purpose flour

2 tsp. coarse salt

1 ½ Tbsp. Saf-instant yeast

2 cups water *(about 110 degrees F)*

1 whole egg

1 egg beaten for wash

Utensils:
Large bowl
Floured board
Cookie sheet
Sharp Knife

Preparation time: 30 minutes
Oven temp: 375°F
Baking time: 15 - 20 minutes or until golden
Results: 4 loaves

Instructions:

1. **Place all ingredients into mixing bowl, putting the water in last. Mix into a dough and turn out onto floured board. Knead for about 10 minutes. Allow the dough to rest until it has doubled in size.**

2. **Divide the dough into 4 pieces and form them into loaves. Brush the loaves with egg wash and make slits in the top of each loaf. Allow loaves to rest about 20 minutes and bake them at 375°F for 15 - 20 minutes until golden.**

Bonnie's Banana Loaf

Ingredients:

2 cups sugar

1 cup butter *(soft, 2 sticks)*

2 whole eggs

4 very ripe bananas, *(black is great)*

2 ½ cups unbleached all-purpose flour

1 ½ tsp. baking soda

1 tsp. salt

2 cups walnuts *(optional)*

Utensils:
Large bowl
2 standard bread
pans greased and
floured

Preparation time: 30 minutes
Oven temp: 375°F
Baking time: Until center appears firm
approximately 45 minutes
Results: 2 loaves

Instructions:

1. **Cream the butter and sugar until smooth and fluffy.**
2. **Add the eggs and bananas and cream again.**
3. **Add the flour, baking soda, and salt.**
4. **Pour the batter into greased and floured bread pans or non-stick muffin pans.**
5. **Bake at 375°F until the center appears firm approximately 45 minutes.**

Zesty Herb Bread

Ingredients:

Dough
4 cups high gluten flour
1 ½ cups warm water
   (about 90 – 100 degrees)
½ tsp. salt
1 Tbsp. granulated sugar
1 Tbsp. salad oil
1 whole egg
1 ½ Tbsp. Saf-instant yeast
4 Tbsp. herb mix
½ cup yellow cornmeal to
   sprinkle on pan

Herb Mix
4 Tbsp. parmesan cheese,
   finely grated
2 Tbsp. oregano
1 Tbsp. sweet basil
2 Tbsp. chives or onion
1 tsp. thyme
½ tsp. black pepper
1 tsp. paprika
1 Tbsp. garlic salt or garlic
   powder

Egg Wash
One egg white beaten

Utensils:
Large bowl
Tight sealing jar
Floured board
Baking sheet sprinkled
   with cornmeal

Preparation time: 30 minutes
Oven temp. 400°F
Baking time: About 25 minutes or
   until golden
Results: 2 loaves

Instructions:

1. Mix together herbs and seal in a tight jar.
2. Mix the flour, sugar, oil, egg, salt, yeast, and 4 Tbsp. of the herb mix into a straight dough, adding the water last.
3. Turn onto a floured board and knead for 10 minutes, adding a small amount of water if necessary.
4. Allow dough to rest for 10 minutes, then divide into 2 halves and shape loaves. Place on baking sheet that has been sprinkled with corn meal.
5. Lightly brush with egg white.
6. Put loaves into a warm place and allow them to rise until they double in size.
7. Preheat oven to 400°F. Bake loaves for about 25 minutes or until golden. When fully baked, the loaves will have a hollow sound when tapped. Serve warm.

The Fire Will Be There
When We Get There

When I was growing up during the Cold War, my dad was the Civil Defense Warden for the town of St. Johnsbury. He was also the chief call man for the St. Johnsbury Fire Department for nearly 50 years.

He used to head out to fires in The Gray Ghost, which had a flashing light on the roof with two domes – a yellow one for plowing and a red one to go to fires. Sometimes, he would have to change the dome from yellow to red before heading to a fire!

As a kid, I sometimes got to go along with him when there was a fire call. And I remember that it all seemed very slow as he put on his fire coat and as we drove along in The Gray Ghost, which had a top speed of about 45 miles an hour.

I was always excited and remember one day saying, "Dad, can't you go any faster?"

He responded, "Well, the fire will be there when we get there." And we always did manage to get there and the firemen would always get the fire out.

But it sure seemed slow to a kid!

Ingredients:

5 cups unbleached all-purpose flour

2 cups dark rye flour

1 ½ cups dried sour cherries

1 Tbsp. + 1 tsp. kosher salt

3 Tbsp. Saf-instant yeast

3 cups warm water *(about 110 degrees F)*

Utensils:
Large bowl
Floured board
Cookie sheet
Sharp knife

Preparation time: 30 minutes
Oven temp: 375°F
Baking time: 15 - 20 minutes or until golden
Results: 2 loaves

Instructions:

1. **Place all the ingredients into mixing bowl, adding the water last. Mix into a dough, turn out onto a lightly floured board, and knead for about 6 minutes. Allow the dough to rest until doubled in size.**

2. **Divide the dough in half and form each half into a loaf. Brush each loaf with beaten egg and lightly score the top with a sharp knife. Allow to double in size and bake at 375°F for 15 - 20 minutes or until golden and crusty.**

Walnut Bread

Ingredients:

2 Tbsp. Saf-instant yeast

1 Tbsp. light brown sugar

1 Tbsp. canola oil

6 cups all-purpose flour

2 cups walnut pieces

1 egg yoke

1 tsp. kosher or sea salt

2 ½ cups warm water *(about 110 degrees F)*

Utensils:
Large bowl

Two standard bread
  pans greased and
  floured

Preparation time: 20 minutes

Oven temp: 375°F

Baking time: Approximately 30 minutes

Results: 2 loaves

Instructions:

1. **Place all ingredients in large bowl, putting water in last.**
2. **Mix into dough, then knead for 10 minutes.**
3. **Divide dough in half and place into 2 greased and floured bread pans.**
4. **Brush with melted butter and allow dough to rest in a warm plce until double in size.**
5. **Bake at 375°F for approximately 30 minutes**

Herb Flat Bread for Dipping

Ingredients:

Dough

3 ½ cups all-purpose flour
1 ½ cups rye flour
½ cup warm milk
  (about 110 degrees)
2 cups warm water
  (about 110 degrees)
½ tsp. sugar
1 Tbsp. Saf-instant yeast
1 tsp. salt
4 tsp. herb mix
½ cup yellow cornmeal
  to sprinkle on pan

Herb Mix

4 Tbsp. parmesan cheese,
  finely grated
2 Tbsp. oregano
1 Tbsp. sweet basil
2 Tbsp. chives or onion
1 tsp. thyme
½ tsp. black pepper
1 tsp. paprika
1 Tbsp. garlic salt
  or garlic powder

Egg Wash

1 egg white beaten

Utensils:

Large bowl
Tight sealing jar
Floured board
Baking sheet sprinkled
  with cornmeal

Preparation time: 30 minutes
Oven temp: 375°F
Baking time: About 15 - 20 minutes
Results: 8 flatbreads

Instructions:

1. **Mix together herbs and seal in a tight jar.**
2. **Mix the water, milk, sugar, and yeast in large bowl and let stand for 5 minutes.**
3. **Add all remaining ingredients and mix into a straight dough.**
4. **Knead for about 8 minutes.**
5. **Allow dough to rest for 10 minutes, then divide into 8 parts and roll out into ¼ inch thick circles. Brush lightly with egg white and sprinkle with all-purpose flour.**
6. **Put loaves into a warm place and allow them to rise until they double in size.**
7. **Preheat oven to 375°F. Bake loaves for about 15 - 20 minutes. Cool and serve plain or with fresh salsa or spinach dip.**

Fill 'er Up Mister?

My dad, Gerald Faye, owned a Shell filling station and auto repair shop in St. Johnsbury and was a hard worker. This was in the days when a gas station had a machine shop in back and he could keep cars running no matter what. During the war years, he made parts and kept cars on the road when there were no parts. We even used to rebuild car batteries.

When I grew up, I had to work in the gas station after school and on weekends. I remember that on the first day I worked pumping gas, it was

26 cents a gallon! As a teenager, I also worked in the shop doing brake jobs, lube jobs, oil changes, and making wrecker calls. I handled all kinds of repairs.

In those days, when you went in to get a grease job and oil change, you got your car vacuumed out and the windows washed. And that was called full service. Dad would line up all his lube jobs and oil changes in the afternoons so that when I got home from school, there was always a row of seven or eight cars that I had to vacuum and clean windows before dinner.

When I was a sophomore in high school, my dad had a heart attack and for a while wasn't able to work. My mother was in a wheelchair and wasn't very well, so I had to quit school for a while and run the garage. That winter I worked all day in the garage and then plowed snow at night to keep food on the table until my dad could get back to work.

I kept up with my school work by studying on the old desk at the filling station after I had taken the pump readings and closed up. My mother helped me, too, because she had been a fine teacher and had taught three generations of students. So I was able to keep up my grades and graduate on time.

My dad got back to work after a few months and he worked in the garage until he was 72. One day he said, "That's that." He closed the garage, packed up his tools, and went home. I had always thought I would take over the garage when he retired, but suddenly I found I needed to find a new way to make a living.

The old Gerald Faye garage building is still standing at 1 Concord Avenue in St. Johnsbury.

Tuscan Style Rosemary & Raisin Bread

Ingredients:

½ cup water *(about 110 degrees F)*

4 cups all-purpose flour

2 Tbsp. powdered milk

1 ½ tsp. salt

1 ½ cups raisins

1 Tbsp. fresh rosemary leaves

¼ cup olive oil

4 large eggs *(beaten)*

1 Tbsp. Saf-instant yeast

Utensils:
Large bowl
Floured board
Cookie sheet
Sharp knife

Preparation time: 30 minutes
Oven temp: 400°F
Baking time: 35 - 45 minutes or until golden
Results: 2 loaves

Instructions:

1. **Place all ingredients in large bowl, putting water in last.**

2. **Mix to soft dough and turn out onto lightly floured board.**

3. **Knead 10 minutes, cover and allow to double in size.**

4. **Divide into two loaves, round up and place on 2 cookie sheets.**

5. **Brush with egg wash.**

6. **Let rise again.**

7. **Slit across the top with sharp knife and bake at 400°F for 35 - 45 minutes until golden.**

Breakfast On The Go Bread

Ingredients:

6 cups all-purpose flour

$1/2$ cup granulated sugar

1 $1/2$ Tbsp. Saf-instant yeast

$1/4$ cup butter (*$1/2$ stick*)

2 $1/2$ tsp. salt

3 cups warm milk

3 tsp. vanilla

1 tsp. rum

Utensils:
Large bowl
Floured board
Two large floured and greased bread pans

Preparation time: 45 minutes
Oven temp: 375°F
Baking time: 45 - 60 minutes
Results: 5 + dozen

Instructions:

1. Place all ingredients in large bowl, putting milk in last.
2. Mix into dough, place on floured board, then knead for 10 minutes.
3. Divide dough in half. Cut each half into 32 pieces
4. Roll each piece into a ball and then roll each ball in melted butter and cinnamon sugar mix.
5. Pack into 2 large bread pans and let rise to double the size.
6. Bake at 375°F for 45 - 60 minutes

Ingredients:

4 cups whole wheat flour

1 ½ Tbsp. Saf-instant yeast

2 cups warm water *(about 110 degrees)*

½ cup Vermont honey

2 Tbsp. melted butter

Utensils:

Large bowl

Floured board

9 inch Bread loaf pans,
  lightly oiled

Preparation time: 15 minutes

Oven temp: 350°F

Baking time: About 45 minutes

Results: 2 loaves

Instructions:

1. Place warm water in a bowl.
2. Add flour, honey, and yeast and mix into straight dough.
3. Turn out dough onto floured board. Knead lightly for 5 minutes.
4. Form into two loaves and put in lightly oiled 9 inch bread pans.
5. Allow to rise for 20 minutes, then bake at 350°F for about 45 minutes or until golden brown.
6. Brush melted butter on top of bread while it is still hot from the oven.

Camp: A Vermont Tradition

In 1918 my dad mustered out of the First World War where he served as a member of the First Vermont Militia.

Right after he got out, he built a deer camp on a brook in a remote part of Maidstone in Vermont's Northeast Kingdom. Eighty-four years later, the camp hasn't changed much. Many of my earliest memories are of times spent at camp and my own kids' earliest memories are of camp.

For people who have never seen a deer camp, most of them aren't very pretty. Some aren't much bigger than the tool sheds that suburbanites have in their back yards. Camps tend to be way up in the

North Woods. No indoor plumbing. Though many now have some kind of electric lights, mine still has no electricity. We cook on a big old wood stove and relax by lantern-light in the evenings – the same as my father did in the 1920s. There's nothing luxurious about it, but when you get back after a long day in the woods, it's pretty inviting.

There is a misconception that everyone goes to deer camp to get drunk and party, but that's the exception rather than the rule. Our camp has a pretty strict code and has always been a camp for real woodsmen. Nobody can have a drink until all the guns are cleaned and put away and even then, there's no heavy drinking allowed because we are all out in the woods before daybreak, heading up the mountains after deer.

The most fascinating thing about our camp is the walls. The walls are insulated with layers of cardboard put up by my father years ago. And all over the walls, people have written the history of the camp: every visit, every new person, every milestone, every deer we have taken, every trout we have caught, and every bear we have seen. All have been written on the walls of the camp for more than 80 years. One notation that stands out is from 1920: "Drove to camp in car." That was a first. Almost a century of change has been recorded on those walls.

Deer camp was my wife Bonnie's favorite place in the world. Not long before she passed away, I asked her what she would like to do special for Thanksgiving. She said that she would like to go up to camp. There was a lot of snow on the ground, but we spent the week at the camp hunting together in the mountains and enjoying the woods. Thanksgiving dinner was a steak cooked  on an open fire in the pit outside the camp. I cooked all the trimmings on the wood stove. My son and daughter came up and we had a family Thanksgiving dinner together at the camp. No luxury resort could have compared to the time we had that Thanksgiving.

I'll never tire of going to deer camp.

I Can Get Turned Around In My Back Yard

Everyone thinks that a Vermont woodsman should have a perfect sense of direction.

I don't. I am lost constantly when I am in the woods. In fact, I could get turned around in my back yard. If I don't use my compass, I'll end up walking around in a circle just about anywhere.

The worst I ever got lost was in Maidstone. I was on Burnside Mountain which is tricky because it looks the same on both sides. So if you don't pay attention you might find you are going down the wrong side. My father had always told me to look at the stream at the base of the mountain. If the water flowed from left to right, I was ok. If the stream flowed right to left, I was in trouble and had to go back over the mountain or risk getting lost in the Victory-Granby Bog.

This particular day I got down to the bottom and found the water running the wrong way. To make matters worse, it was almost dark and I didn't want to go back over the mountain. But I figured if I followed the brook, I could be in camp in about three hours. What I didn't count on was a string of beaver ponds and then a swamp. Next thing I knew I was completely lost – basically just walking in the woods. And it was pitch dark.

Finally, I found a path. I followed the path to the left and it started up a steep hill, so I went the other way. Suddenly, in the middle of the Vermont woods, I smelled mothballs and I knew exactly where I was.

I was on the access path to the Stone Mountain fire tower in Victory. The ground was littered with mothballs that the fire warden would put around his car to keep the porcupines from chewing the tires off!

By about 11:30, I got onto the Victory-Granby Road and knocked on the door of a camp. They invited me in and fed me venison stew. No stew before or since has ever tasted that good. Later, they drove me back to my camp in Maidstone.

I was some tired that night!

Light Rye Bread

Ingredients:

4 cups all-purpose flour
2 cups dark rye flour
¼ cup rye chops *(optional)*
1 Tbsp. caraway seeds *(optional)*
2 ¾ cups warm water *(110 degrees)*
1 Tbsp. molasses
1 Tbsp. vegetable oil
2 Tbsp. Saf-instant yeast
1 tsp. salt
½ cup cornmeal sprinkled on baking sheet
1 egg white, beaten, to brush onto loaf

Utensils:	Preparation time: 30 minutes
Large bowl	Oven temp: 400°F
Floured board	Baking time: About 40 minutes
Baking sheet sprinkled with	or until golden brown
cornmeal	Results: 2 loaves
Sharp knife	

Instructions:

1. Place bread, flour, rye flour, rye chops, molasses, and vegetable oil in bowl. Add water and mix lightly. Add yeast last and mix into a straight dough.
2. Turn onto a floured board and knead for 10 minutes.
3. Divide into two halves and allow to rest for 10 minutes.
4. Shape into round loaves. Flatten dough slightly on baking sheet that has been sprinkled with corn meal.
5. Lightly brush loaves with beaten egg and sprinkle with caraway seeds if desired.
6. Put loaves into a warm place and allow them to rise until loaves double in size.
7. Preheat oven to 400°F. For the first 10 minutes, spritz water into oven every 2 - 3 minutes with a sprayer to create steam.
8. Continue to bake for 40 minutes until golden colored. When fully baked, the loaves will have a hollow sound when tapped. Serve warm and slice at table or slice thin for sandwiches.

Coming Of Age In Vermont:
My First Deer

In Vermont in the '50s, there were only a few events that you would consider milestones. Your first kiss. Your driver's license. Becoming a Scout. Your first deer rifle. Of course, one event eclipsed all the others by a mile: your first buck!

I started hunting and fishing as soon as I was old enough to hold a fishing rod and safely handle a rifle. For many years, while I was learning my way around the woods, I would follow my dad up in the

mountains. And after a while, I was given a Winchester 25-20 rifle and allowed to hunt with him.

When I was eleven years old, we were hunting up in Maidstone. We were hiking up the mountain and he'd go a ways and stop so I could catch up with him. As soon as I caught up, he would go on again. Of course, he was stopping to rest but he was walking me until I thought I was going to die!

That day we got up near the top of a mountain called Roundtop, arriving just at the break of dawn. We were standing almost shoulder-to-shoulder when we heard a deer and looked up. This deer was coming down an old tote-road heading right at us.

My dad certainly was looking forward to the day when his son would get his first deer. But not if it kept him from filling his buck tag that season! So we both fired at the same time.

He missed. I didn't.

Mediterranean Bread

Ingredients:
6 cups all-purpose flour
2 ¼ cups warm water *(about 110 degrees)*
2 Tbsp. olive oil
1 Tbsp. salt
¾ cup chopped ripe olives
¾ cup chopped sundried tomatoes
1 Tbsp. finely chopped fresh garlic
3 Tbsp. Saf-instant yeast
1 Tbsp. coarse salt or sea salt

Utensils:
Large bowl
Floured board
Baking sheet, lightly
  brushed with olive oil
Sharp knife

Preparation time: 30 minutes
Oven temp: 420°F
Baking time: About 25 - 30 minutes
Results: 2 loaves with
  6 pieces each

Instructions:
1. **Place yeast, oil, flour, and salt in a bowl. Stir together lightly.**
2. **Add water and remaining ingredients. Mix into straight dough and turn out dough onto floured board.**
3. **Knead for 8 minutes. Cover and put in a warm place to rise for 20 minutes.**
4. **Divide in half and flatten each piece into a rectangle about ½ inch thick. Cut 4 to 6 slits in each piece and stretch apart slightly.**
5. **Place on baking sheet that has been lightly brushed with olive oil. Brush loaves with olive oil and sprinkle with coarse salt or sea salt.**
6. **Allow to rise again for 10 minutes. Preheat oven to 420°F and bake loaves for 25 - 30 minutes or until crust is golden and crisp. Tear and serve with hummus or plain.**

Scared Straight

I had only one brush with the law when I was growing up. I was 16 and not too smart about some things.

My father, who owned the local garage and had a wonderful sense of humor, showed me how to weld a spark plug in the tailpipe of the car and then wire it to a battery and a coil in the trunk. You could then shut off your ignition for a few seconds while you were driving and the engine would dump a whole lot of raw gas into the exhaust.

Then when you turned your ignition back on, the engine would start again and the plug in the tailpipe would light the gas. Instant cannon/flamethrower! Flames would shoot for 30 feet out the back of the car!

One morning on my way to school, I decided to wake up the town of

St. Johnsbury with my automotive flamethrower. What I hadn't noticed was that one of the St. Johnsbury police officers was right behind me – headed to work in his own brand new car! Needless to say, the flames did quite a number on the front end of his car and I was busted big time!

So I had to go to court with my parents. My mother cried and my father was mad. The judge pounded his gavel. A lawyer friend of my father's kept things from getting out of hand. It was an interesting scene and not one I ever wanted to repeat. In the end, I had to work to pay the fine and write a 5,000 word essay on law enforcement. I also had to visit the local jail to see what was in store for me if I ever crossed the line again.

One good thing to come out of that episode was that the sheriff who ran the jail became one of my best friends. I found whole new empathy for police officers because of that!

To this day, many of our local police officers are among my best friends.

Ingredients:

3 cups all-purpose flour
1 cup wheat bran
2 cups whole wheat flour
3 Tbsp. Saf-instant yeast
2 cups warm water *(about 110 degrees)*
$1/4$ cup *(1/2 stick)* butter
2 cups mushrooms, finely chopped
1 cup onion, finely chopped
3 Tbsp. molasses
1 egg
White from one egg, beaten, to brush on loaves

Utensils:

Large bowl
Floured board
Two 9 inch bread loaf pans,
  lightly greased

Preparation time: 20 minutes

Oven temp: 375°F
Baking time: About 35 - 40 minutes
  or until golden brown
Results: 2 loaves

Instructions:

1. **Place all the ingredients in a large bowl, adding water last.**
2. **Work into a straight dough and turn onto floured board.**
3. **Knead 5 minutes.**
4. **Divide into two and form into loaves.**
5. **Place loaves into greased bread pans and brush with egg white.**
6. **Set in a warm place until loaves double in size.**
7. **Preheat oven to 375°F and bake for 35 - 40 minutes until golden brown. Serve warm.**

Pain au Chocolate
(Chocolate Bread)

Ingredients:
3 ⅓ cups all-purpose flour
1 cup (2 sticks) softened butter
4 eggs
½ tsp. salt
2 Tbsp. Saf-instant yeast
½ cup warm milk (about 110 degrees)
1 tsp. sugar
2 cups chocolate chips
1 egg yolk to brush on loaves

Utensils:
Large bowl
Floured board
Buttered non-stick
  baking sheet

Preparation time: 45 minutes
Oven temp: 375°F
Baking time: About 25 minutes
Results: 16 mini-loaves

Instructions:

1. Place all ingredients, except chocolate chips and egg yolk, in a large bowl and mix into a straight dough.

2. Place on floured board and knead for 10 minutes.

3. Allow dough to rest for 10 minutes then divide into half and then into 8 equal pieces for a total of 16 pieces.

4. Flatten pieces of dough and place about 1 tablespoon of chocolate chips on each piece. Fold the dough over and pinch the edges closed, sealing the chips inside.

5. Place on a lightly buttered non-stick baking pan, brush lightly with egg yolk and allow to rise for about 30 minutes.

6. Preheat oven to 375°F. Bake loaves for about 25 minutes. Serve warm, allowing the filling to cool.

Pain du Champagne
(French Country Bread)

Starter:

1 Tbsp. Saf-instant yeast

2 cups warm water
  (about 110 degrees)

1 cup warm milk
  (about 110 degrees)

1 cup flour

3 tsp. cider vinegar

Mix together and allow to stand at room temperature for at least two days.

Replace any starter removed with flour wash made from a 50/50 water and flour mix.

Ingredients:

4 cups unbleached all-purpose flour

³/₄ cup white or dark rye flour

³/₄ cup whole wheat flour

1 cup starter

2 cups warm water *(about 110 degrees)*

1 Tbsp. salt

2 Tbsp. instant yeast

One egg white, beaten, to brush on loaves

¹/₂ cup yellow corn meal for sprinkling on baking pans

Utensils:

Large bowl

Floured board

Baking sheet, lightly greased

Sharp knife

Preparation time: 45 minutes
(spread over three days)

Oven temp: 375°F

Baking time: About 25 - 35 minutes or until golden brown

Results: 2 loaves

Instructions:

1. Place all the ingredients, except egg white and corn meal, in a large bowl and work into a straight dough.
2. Turn onto floured board and knead for about 10 minutes.
3. Allow to rise until it doubles in size and then re-knead to knock down rise.
4. Cut in half and form into two long oval loaves. Place on corn meal on baking sheet. Brush with egg white and sprinkle with all-purpose flour. Make several shallow cuts in top of the loaves.
5. Preheat oven to 375°F and bake for 25 - 35 minutes until golden brown. Serve warm.

"I'll Give You $200 A Month More"

When my dad was 72 he closed the garage, brought his tools home, and informed me, "You need to find a new way to make a living."

Well, I was seventeen, just graduated from high school and all I knew how to do was work on cars and tractors and equipment. I had always assumed that I would take over my dad's garage. My dad had other ideas, I guess.

A friend of mine had gotten a job that summer at Mount Washington in New Hampshire. He loved it and said that I should apply for a job. So I drove my beat-up '53 Ford to Mount Washington and interviewed with the Teague family. Arthur Teague hired me to work as a maintenance man and that summer I lived and worked at the Mount Washington Summit house on the top of the mountain.

One night I was called to the kitchen to fix a gas leak and while I was working, one of the cooks got angry with the chef and quit on the spot. The chef turned to me and told me to put an apron on and help him finish the night. I had cooked while growing up and in the Boy Scouts and at deer camp, so I sort of knew my way around a kitchen. I helped him get through the night and after the shift was over, he asked me if I would leave the maintenance crew and go to work for him in the kitchen.

I told him that I wasn't sure. I kind of liked the rugged part of being outdoors on top of the mountain and working on machinery and fixing things.

He said, "I'll give you $200 a month more." Well, on the maintenance crew, I was only making $225 a month, plus board and room. And in the busy summer season, that meant working a seven day week!

Needless to say, I didn't have to think about that long. I just blurted out, "You got yourself a cook!"

Ciabatta Bread

Ingredients:

1 cup Kalamata olives, pitted

²/₃ cup olive oil

¹/₂ tsp. lemon zest

2 tsp. fresh thyme, chopped

5 cups all-purpose flour

2 ¹/₂ tsp. kosher or sea salt

2 Tbsp. Saf-instant yeast

2 cups water *(about 110 degrees F)*

Utensils:

Large bowl

Cookie sheet,
    papered

Preparation time: 30 minutes

Oven temp: 425°F

Baking time: 30 minutes or until golden

Results: 2 loaves

Instructions:

1. Place all ingredients in large bowl, adding water last.

2. Mix to straight dough.

3. Let rise to double in size.

4. Divide and shape into 2 rectangles approximately 12 inches long.

5. Place on papered cookie sheet, dust with flour, and allow to rise again.

6. Bake at 425°F for about 30 minutes or until golden.

Short Stories From the Bakery

Be Careful What You Say

When Big Ben was my bakery assistant manager I learned what not to say. As I was leaving work after a particularly long day, my parting comment, in jest, was, "Anyone want to kiss me good-bye?"
Before I could get away Ben grabbed me in a bear-hug (no mercy) and gave me a sweaty-wiskery, Marlboro scented kiss. To say it was a terrifying moment would be an under statement. I've never said THAT again ! ! !

The Customer is Always Right

One snowy day in February a gentleman arrived at the bakery for coffee and directions for driving to the Von Trapp chapel. The person waiting on him gave him directions, but let him know that it was a footpath or ski trail that would lead him to the chapel. His answer was, "but I have an Audi". Overhearing the exchange, I tactfully confirmed my employee's message. His reply to me also, was, "but I have an Audi", and off he went. Now I have to admit, that Audi's are amazing autos, but aren't equipped with skis. A short time later our snow-cat operator was called to retrieve a new car that was buried off one of the ski trails, near the chapel.

We Always Please Our Guests

I once took an order for a birthday cake from one of our guests. It was for her young daughter. She requested that I make it taste like a supermarket cake, with frosting that tasted like that from a can. It was the only kind of cake her daughter liked. I did my best . . . but talk about testing a pastry chef's skills ! ! !

Soft Wheat Dinner Rolls

Ingredients:
2 ½ cups warm water *(about 110 degrees)*
½ cup milk powder
1 whole egg
1 tsp. salt
½ cup granulated sugar
½ cup vegetable shortening
6 cups all-purpose flour
1 cup whole wheat flour
1 cup cracked wheat
¾ oz. Saf-instant yeast *(about 2 Tbsp.)*
1 egg beaten

Utensils:
Large bowl
Floured board

Preparation time: 45 minutes
Oven temp: 375°F
Baking time: About 20 minutes or until lightly
  golden brown
Results: Two dozen rolls

Instructions:

1. **Place flour, milk powder, salt, sugar, shortening, cracked wheat, and yeast into a large bowl. Add water and one egg into the mixture.**

2. **Work into dough and then place on floured board.**

3. **Knead for 10 minutes and allow the dough to rest for 20 minutes.**

4. **Pat out dough to 1 inch thick and cut into desired size rolls, keeping in mind that they will double in size! Squares about 1 ½ inches are ideal.**

5. **Pat gently, roll, shape, and place on greased and floured baking pan.**

6. **Brush gently with beaten egg.**

7. **Let rise in a warm place until rolls double in size.**

8. **Preheat oven to 375°F and bake for about 20 minutes or until lightly golden. Serve hot from the oven.**

Life In The CIA

When I got the new cooking job at Mount Washington, I wrote my mother to tell her what had happened and that I was in the kitchen cooking.

She wrote back that she had heard from a friend about a cooking school in New Haven, Connecticut where they took veterans and other people and taught them how to be chefs. My mother suggested that if I liked cooking, maybe I could go to college there and learn to be a professional chef.

So with some prompting from my parents, I left the employ of Mount Washington and drove down to New Haven and enrolled in the Culinary Institute of America. This was before they had moved to Hyde Park and they were at 300 Prospect Street in New Haven.

Though a lot of the students were attending the CIA on the GI Bill, I had to work my way through. So whenever I wasn't in class or preparing my assignments, I was working. I washed glasses in a bar. I was a security guard. I peddled milk for a dairy. And I worked for restaurants cooking and washing dishes. For a while I was even driving my old Ford to New Jersey every weekend to work for a resort. Any way to make money.

My time at the CIA was my first exposure to the real world.

Sweet Oatmeal Bread
(As Featured in *Gourmet* Magazine)

Ingredients:
5 cups all-purpose flour
2 ozs. (*¹/₂ stick*) salted butter
¹/₂ cup dark brown sugar, packed
¹/₂ tsp. salt
1 ¹/₂ cups oatmeal
2 ¹/₂ cups warm water *(about 110 degrees)*
1 ¹/₂ Tbsp. Saf-instant yeast
1 egg white, beaten, to brush on loaves
¹/₂ cup oatmeal to sprinkle on loaves

Utensils:
Large bowl
Floured board
Baking sheet, lightly oiled

Preparation time: 30 minutes
Oven temp: 375°F
Baking time: About 30 minutes
Results: 2 loaves

Instructions:
1. Mix the butter, brown sugar, and oatmeal in a large bowl.
2. Pour in the water and let stand for 3 minutes.
3. Add remaining ingredients, except the egg white, and mix into a dough, kneading for 10 minutes.
4. Allow dough to rest for 15 minutes then turn out onto floured board. Divide into two halves and shape into loaves.
5. Lightly brush with beaten egg and sprinkle with oatmeal then place on baking sheet.
6. Put loaves into a warm place and allow them to rise until they double in size.
7. Preheat oven to 375°F. Bake for about 30 minutes. Serve warm.

Two Chefs For The Price Of One

For a kid from St. Johnsbury, cooking school was the opportunity of a lifetime. And I just grabbed the brass ring!

Even with all the time I had to spend working for my tuition, I became the only graduate who actually was able to work three years of classes into two years. Halfway through my second year, I had completed my two years' curriculum and I was bored.

So I went to the dean and begged him to let me take the baking course because I wanted to learn to be a baker and pastry chef as well as a continental chef. The dean thought about it and agreed to let me take the baking course with the stipulation that if I failed it, I wouldn't get a degree in anything. But if I passed, I could have both degrees.

For six months I worked really hard to learn a year's worth of baking.

I sweated the final exam. The final involved creating a complete bake shop full of pastries – enough for the entire school – in one night. Then you had to clean up the bakery before morning when all the instructor-chefs came in and judged what you had made. It was a pass or fail situation and not everybody passed.

After the judges finished, they lined up on the walk leading up to the Jacob Tanner Memorial Bake Shop and summoned me back. I walked down the path looking at the chefs who had very stern and serious expressions. I was very nervous too, thinking, "Must be they didn't like it. I'm in trouble."

Then bakery instructors Joseph Scheiss and Joe Amidola broke out of the group and walked up to me with big smiles and said, "Well, Woodchuck, you are one of the number one students in our class. It was beautiful." They all shook my hand and said it was one of the best jobs they had seen in several years.

I graduated from CIA number one in my class and I earned both degrees. I received a lot of awards for being the top student in baking.

Though I received the A.J. Spiler award for Excellence in Baking, the biggest award of all was when my two mentors – Joseph Scheiss and Joseph Amidola – walked out of the ranks of chefs the morning of the exam to shake my hand.

Vienna Braided Bread

Ingredients:
1 ½ cups warm water *(about 90 - 110 degrees)*
1 quart all-purpose flour
1 Tbsp. granulated sugar
1 Tbsp. olive oil
1 whole egg
1 ½ Tbsp. Saf-instant yeast
Sesame seeds or poppy seeds, if desired
½ cup yellow cornmeal

Utensils:
Large bowl
Floured board
Baking sheet
   sprinkled
   with cornmeal

Preparation time: 20 minutes
Oven temp: 400°F
Baking time: About 25 minutes
   or until golden
Results: 2 loaves

Instructions:
1. Mix the water, flour, sugar, oil, and egg into a straight dough, adding the yeast last.
2. Turn onto a floured board and knead for 10 minutes, adding a small amount of water if necessary.
3. Allow dough to rest for 10 minutes, then divide into 6 equal pieces. Roll each piece into a rope about 12 inches long. Braid three ropes together to make each loaf.
4. If desired, brush with beaten egg and then sprinkle with poppy seeds or sesame seeds.
5. Put loaves into a warm place and allow them to rise until they double in size.
6. Bake in 400°F oven for about 25 minutes or until golden. When fully baked, the loaves will have a hollow sound when tapped. Serve warm.

Pies, Cakes, and Tarts

"I Gotta Meet This Girl!"

Not long after I graduated from the Culinary Institute, I got a job as the chef at Camp Quinnebec, a girl's camp on Lake Fairlee in Vermont. Though I was a professional chef, I was only about 20, so a summer job at a girl's camp was a pretty good first job. As a bonus, I was able to fish a lot when I wasn't overseeing the kitchen.

Not long after the season started, one of the boys whom I had hired to work in the kitchen was showing off for the girls by doing handstands on a stone wall. He fell and broke his collarbone and had to

leave the camp. I put out the word to the counselors that if any of them were interested, I was looking to hire another kitchen helper.

That same evening, I was down at the lake after dinner doing some fishing. Just down the shore was a girl standing on a rock at the edge of the lake, plugging for bass. That intrigued me because, especially in those days, you didn't often see women fishing. I said to myself, "I gotta meet this girl. I don't know who she is, but any girl who's bass fishing down here, I've got to find out more about!"

The next day, she was one of the applicants to work in my kitchen.

Naturally, I hired her on the spot. And it turned out she was the hardest worker on the crew.

Alphen Alfel Cake
(Mountain Apple Cake)

Ingredients:

Cake

2 eggs
1 cup vegetable oil
1 tsp. vanilla
2 cups sugar
2 cups all-purpose flour
2 tsp. cinnamon
1 tsp. baking soda
$\frac{1}{2}$ tsp. salt
4 cups thin-sliced Vermont
　apples *(about 4 large apples)*
1 cup chopped walnuts

Optional Icing

6 oz. cream cheese
6 Tbsp. *(½ stick)* melted butter
1 tsp. vanilla
2 ½ cups confectioners sugar

Utensils:

Large bowl
Flour sifter
Two 8" cake pans

Preparation time: 25 minutes
Oven temp: 350°F
Baking time: 30 minutes
Results: 2 single-layer cakes

Instructions:

1. **Beat eggs and oil until frothy. Add sugar and vanilla and beat again. Add flour, cinnamon, soda, and salt slowly while mixing.**

2. **Stir in apples and walnuts, mixing until evenly distributed.**

3. **Turn batter into two greased and floured cake pans.**

4. **Preheat oven to 350°F and bake for about 30 minutes until cakes are springy to the touch.**

5. **While cakes are cooling, make icing by mixing together the cream cheese and butter, beating until creamy. Add vanilla and confectioners sugar and beat until smooth.**

6. **Drizzle icing over cooled cakes.**

Giving Them Something To Listen To

Bonnie and I did not hit it off immediately. In fact, for the first half of the summer during which we met, we were pretty adversarial.

I asked her out several times, but she wouldn't give me the time of day. It didn't help that the other girls working at the camp assumed that since I was a chef and I was running the kitchen, I  must be much older. So they kept telling Bonnie, who was 17, to steer clear. But I was only 20 and I had set my sights on getting a date with her, so I kept at it.

Finally, Bonnie agreed to go with me to town and get a creemee at the local ice cream shop. We set off toward the village in my Plymouth Fury.

After a couple of miles, I started to hear a "squeak, squeak, squeak" coming from my car. Having rebuilt the car myself, I knew it didn't normally squeak like that and I pulled over. That made Bonnie very nervous and she had her hand on the door handle. But the squeak was still there. So I shut the car off. And all you could hear was the car's motor ticking from the heat and a little "squeak, squeak, squeak".

I looked at her and said, "All right, what's going on?"

"What do you mean?" she asked innocently. I said that I knew my car intimately well and I *especially* knew that it didn't squeak when it was parked with the engine turned off!

At that point, Bonnie broke down and started giggling and confessed that the girls in the dormitory where she was living had put her up to planting a tape recorder under the seat in my car. They were all hoping that I would put the moves on her and she would be able to play the tape for all of them to laugh at.

That was when I discovered that she had a marvelous sense of humor. So we went on and had a creemee and we made a recording for the girls to listen to. We fished together a lot that summer and spent time on the lake in the camp canoes.

We also ended up married for 33 wonderful years!

Island Coconut Custard Pie

Ingredients:

Crust
3 cups all-purpose flour
2 cups vegetable shortening
1 cup cold water
1 tsp. salt

Filling
2 cups toasted coconut
9 eggs
3 cups milk
2 tsp. vanilla
1 cup light brown sugar, packed

Utensils:
Large bowl
Floured board
Rolling pin
Two 9 inch pie pans, greased

Preparation time: 35 minutes
Oven temp: 375°F
Baking time: About 30 minutes
Results: 2 pies

Instructions:

1. Start with the crust, mixing the flour and shortening together until crumbly. Do not overmix!

2. Add cold water and salt. Mix just enough to make a smooth pastry. Let pastry rest for at least 5 minutes. It can be refrigerated at this point.

3. Divide pastry into quarters and set aside two quarters. Use the other two quarters to roll out two open crust pie shells. Put pastry in pie pans and crimp edges.

4. Mix all the filling ingredients together until smooth. Pour equal amounts into each pie shell.

5. Preheat oven to 375°F and bake about 30 minutes until golden colored and slightly raised. Serve warm or chill and decorate with whipped cream and toasted coconut.

Top with fresh whipped cream made by combining 2 cups heavy cream, ¹/₂ cup granulated sugar, and 1 tsp. vanilla. Whip until fluffy. The extra dough can be used to make Rum Walnuss Horns (See page 113).

Poker Winnings

I asked Bonnie to marry me on Christmas Eve, a year-and-a-half after we met. To my delight she accepted! But I had to come up with a ring!

Being just out of chef's school and working hard to build a reputation, I didn't have a lot of money. In fact, I had about $50 to my name. Like many broke young men at the time, I was paying $5 a week for a diamond chip ring at a local jeweler. I was hoping to pay it off in time for our wedding!

One day I arrived at the jewelry store in Lyndon, Vermont, to make my payment. As I pulled into the lot, my car hit a pothole causing a rattle in the ashtray.

The rattle, I remembered, was caused by a ring I had won in a poker game at Lyndon State College a few months earlier. It had been tossed into the pot to cover a $35 bet. The guy who bet the ring had also won it in a poker game in the Army and he probably thought it was glass. I won the hand and, later that night, tossed the ring into the ashtray of my Plymouth Fury. I didn't give it another thought.

But since I was at the jewelry store, I figured the jeweler might be able to tell me what I had.   I fished it out of the ashtray, brushed it off and brought it in to the jeweler, telling him the story of how I got it. I also told him that it had spent months in my ashtray. The jeweler cleaned it up a little and then asked if he could remove the stone from the setting, which I told him was fine. When he looked at it, his jaw dropped.

It turned out to be an extremely fine diamond, perfectly cut and weighing almost a carat! And the ring itself – a large man's ring – was almost an ounce-and-a-half of 14 carat gold!

The jeweler agreed that in exchange for the gold, he would make me a platinum setting for the diamond and would give me back all the money that I had been paying toward the diamond chip.

So that's how, with fifty bucks to my name, I was able to give Bonnie an $8,000 engagement ring!

Crustless Apfel Pie

Ingredients:
3 whole eggs
2 ³/₄ cups granulated sugar
2 cups all-purpose flour
1 ½ tsp. salt
3 tsp. baking powder
2 cups chopped apples
1 ½ cups coarsely chopped walnuts
1 ½ tsp. vanilla

Utensils:
Large bowl
Two 9 inch round pie
 pans, greased

Preparation time: 15 minutes
Oven temp: 350°F
Baking time: 35 minutes
Results: 2 pies

Instructions:

1. In a large bowl, mix the ingredients in order listed above.

2. When thoroughly mixed, pour equally into two greased 9 inch pie pans.

3. Preheat oven to 350°F and bake about 35 minutes until golden and set.

4. Serve warm with ice cream or fresh whipped cream.

Make fresh whipped cream by combining 2 cups heavy cream, ¹/₂ cup granulated sugar, and 1 tsp. vanilla. Whip until fluffy.

Not Only My Wife, But My Best Friend

I had been an outdoors person all my life, so Bonnie and I were pretty much a perfect match.

Bonnie and I met when she was fishing at a summer camp where we both worked. And she was very athletic. She liked to bicycle, hike, snowshoe and ski. She was a state champion gymnast on the trampoline and she liked to ride motorcycles. Though I had grown up in Vermont and hadn't traveled much, Bonnie was a service brat. She had lived all over the world; had gone to school in England. But she was tired of traveling and wanted a life where she could stay in one place.

Soon after we got married, she decided that she wanted to join me in the woods during hunting season.

So she turned out to be not just my wife and my best friend, but also my hunting buddy! In fact, I would rather have gone to camp with Bonnie than with most of the guys I knew because she would hunt hard all day and rarely failed to fill her tag during deer season. She also became an expert shot and never missed. In all her life, she never had to shoot twice to bring down a deer.

And the best part was that I didn't have to worry about her getting lost. I'd always get lost, but Bonnie could find her way back from anywhere.

That lasted all our married life.

Apricot and Almond Tart

Ingredients:

Crust
1 cup light brown sugar
2 cups butter *(soft, 4 sticks)*
1 whole egg
$\frac{1}{2}$ tsp. baking powder
2 tsp. grated orange zest
4 $\frac{1}{2}$ cups all-purpose flour

Filling
$\frac{3}{4}$ cup heavy cream *(also called whipping cream)*
$\frac{3}{4}$ cup granulared sugar
3 whole eggs
1 cup finely ground almonds

2 cups apricot preserves*
Drained canned apricot halves as needed**
1 cup <u>heated</u> apricot preserves***

Utensils:
Large bowl
Two 10 inch cake pans

Preparation time: 25 minutes
Oven temp: 375°F
Baking time: About 30 minutes
Results: 2 tarts

Instructions:

1. Whip all the filling ingredients together and set aside for use in step 3 below.

2. Place all ingredients for crust into large bowl and work into a smooth dough, keeping dough cool. Divide the dough into quarters and press one quarter into bottom of a 10 inch pan and use another quarter to line the pan's sides.

3. Spread 1 cup of apricot preserves* in the bottom of each shell. Place drained canned apricot halves** in the shell, round side up, and pour filling over the apricots.

4. Bake at 375°F until the filling is set *(about 30 minutes)*. Cool slightly and brush the top with strained and heated apricot preserves***.

Mohn Torte
(Christmas Cake)

Ingredients:

3 cups butter *(6 sticks, room temp.)*
12 large eggs
2 cups honey
2 Tbsp. orange zest
2 tsp. vanilla extract
2 cups whole wheat flour
4 cups unbleached flour
2 Tbsp. baking powder
1 tsp. salt
1 ½ cups buttermilk
2 ½ cups sliced almonds
1 cup poppy seeds

Topping
¼ cup confectioners sugar
½ tsp. cinnamon

Utensils:

Large bowl

Two greased and
   floured angel food
   pans or bunt pans

Preparation time: 35 – 45 minutes
Oven temp: 325°F
Baking time: About 35 - 45 minutes
Results: 2 cakes

Instructions:

1. Using large bowl, cream butter adding the eggs one at a time, keeping light as possible. Add honey slowly while creaming. Alternate remaining ingredients and buttermilk until mixture is complete.

2. Pour into 2 greased and floured angel food pans or bunt pans.

3. Bake at 325°F for 35 - 45 minutes until firm or a toothpick comes out clean. Let cool for 20 minutes.

4. Dust with cinnamon and confectioners sugar.

Hungarian Cheese Cake

Ingredients:

Murbteig Crust
½ cup granulated sugar
1 cup (2 *sticks*) butter
3 cups all-purpose flour
½ cup whole eggs
   (2 *large eggs*)
¼ tsp. baking powder
½ cup ground almonds

Topping
¼ cup confectioners
   sugar
½ tsp. cinnamon

Filling
1 ⅓ cup granulated sugar
9 oz. (2 ¼ *sticks*) butter
1 tsp. salt
¼ tsp. vanilla
lemon zest (*to taste*)
1 cup cottage cheese
8 oz. cream cheese
¾ cup all-purpose flour
1 ½ cups whole eggs (6 *large eggs*)
1 cup sour cream
1 cup raisins, soaked in
   Grand Marnier

Utensils:
Large bowl
Floured board
Two 8 inch round pans,
   greased

Preparation time: 35 minutes

Oven temp: 375°F for crust;
   375°F for complete cake

Baking time: 15 minutes for crust;
   40 minutes for complete cake

Results: 2 cheesecakes

Instructions:

1. **Start with the crust, mixing the butter and sugar, beating until creamy.**
2. **Add remaining crust ingredients and work into a smooth dough, keeping it cool as you work it.**
3. **Divide dough in half, then divide each half into thirds. Press ⅔ of the dough into pans. Use leftover dough to make sugar cookies.**
4. **Prebake shells at 375°F for 15 minutes; remove from oven and cool.**
5. **Start the filling by combining the butter, sugar, and cream cheese and beating until creamy. Add salt, vanilla, lemon zest, cottage cheese, and bread flour. Mix smooth.**
6. **Add eggs, sour cream, and raisins. Mix well and pour into shells. Sprinkle with cinnamon sugar.**
7. **Preheat oven to 375°F and bake about 40 minutes until firm and golden colored. Chill and serve cool.**

Stowe, Vermont In The '70s

When I moved here, in the 1970s, Stowe was very different from the town it is today.

By the standards of the day, it was a busy resort town, though there weren't nearly the number of restaurants and hotels that there are today. The Mountain Road, which is now all commercial, still had a lot of working farms on it.

A farm I remember particularly was the Dutton Farm. One day I picked up Mr. Dutton on the side of the road to give him a ride home from a local horse show. When we got back to his farm, he insisted on paying me for the ride by giving me two jars of grape juice that he and his wife made themselves. He farmed well into his '80s.

Another farm on the Mountain Road was the Roberts' dairy farm. Yvon Roberts, who grew up there, became chef at The Trapp Family

Lodge on the same day that I became the baker and pastry chef. I'm still working at the lodge and Yvon retired in December, 2005 as food and beverage director.

Another spot people visiting Stowe will recognize was called Herbie's Pond and that was where we all used to go to swim. Now the pond is part of a big motel and is called "The Commodores Yacht Club" because people race model sailboats on it.

Stowe Village was almost all private homes, though we had three general stores. Harry Walker's IGA was on the south end of Main Street and was a real old-fashioned country store right down to the cheese block and cracker barrel. And there was also the Wells Market and General Store. Shaw's General Store is still on Main Street and at the time it was a true dry-goods store. Today it's a tourist place. But in the '70s, you still went to Shaw's for everything from food to boots; ammunition to farm supplies.

One thing that hasn't changed is Lester Adams' chicken farm, located next to the supermarket on Route 100.

That's still exactly the same as it has been for decades.

Lemon Chess Pie

Ingredients:

Crust
2 cups all-purpose flour
1 cup vegetable shortening
1 tsp. lemon zest
1/2 cup ice water

Filling
3 cups granulated sugar
3/4 cup (1 1/2 sticks) melted butter
7 whole eggs
1 1/3 cups whole milk
1 Tbsp. all-purpose flour
1 Tbsp. yellow cornmeal
1/3 cup lemon juice
2 Tbsp. lemon zest

Utensils:
Large bowl
Floured board
Rolling pin
Two 10 inch pie pans, greased

Preparation time: 35 minutes
Oven temp: 350°F
Baking time: 30 minutes
Results: 2 pies

Instructions:

1. Start with the crust, mixing the flour and shortening together until crumbly. Do not overmix!

2. Add cold water and lemon zest, work quickly into a smooth dough.

3. Divide dough into two pieces and roll out two open crusts, 1/8 inch thick. Put in pie pans and crimp edges.

4. Mix the filling by combining all ingredients and whip until smooth.

5. Pour equal amounts into each pie shell.

6. Preheat oven to 350°F degrees and bake the pies for 30 minutes until golden and set. Allow to cool.

7. Serve chilled and top with whipped cream or serve with ice cream.

Make fresh whipped cream by combining 2 cups heavy cream, 1/2 cup granulated sugar, and 1 tsp. vanilla. Whip until fluffy.

All Our Pets Were Edible

Today, Stowe is a pretty modern resort town. Lots of luxury homes, hotels, and fine dining.

But even in the 1970s when I moved to Stowe, the town was pretty upscale compared to the rest of Vermont. The land I bought to build my house on was $2,000 an acre – which seemed astronomical back then.

Bonnie and I moved into an area of Stowe called Nebraska Valley. The Valley is still one of the few areas of Stowe that hasn't changed much during the past 30 years. Or the past 100 for that matter. There are still some farms; most of the houses are small and simple; and the valley still has a dirt road for most of its length. But even living in this undeveloped part of Stowe was a culture shock for a young man from the Northeast Kingdom.

Of course that was easy to cure. I just brought the Northeast Kingdom to Stowe with me!

Since money was tight, we did what any good Vermont family would do. We raised most of our own food! People don't think of Stowe as a place where you raise your own food, but all our pets were edible. We had pigs, chickens, geese, ducks, rabbits, beef cattle... anything

that was protein. We also canned 200 quarts of produce from our garden every year and stored it in a root cellar we built into our house.

In the fall we would cure our own hams and bacon in a smokehouse I built. In a lot of ways, it was just like the old days when I was growing up in St. J! Bonnie had been far more used to going to the grocery store growing up, but she loved our life in Vermont, even if it meant having to raise dinner.

And fortunately our neighbors were pretty understanding. Even when it came to the pigs.

Whole Wheat Maple Apple Tart

Ingredients:

Whole Wheat Crust

1 ½ cups all-purpose unbleached flour

¾ cup whole wheat flour

1 cup *(two sticks)* butter

1 ⅓ cup brown sugar, tightly packed

1 whole egg

¼ cup Vermont maple syrup for brushing on tart

4 tart apples, peeled, cored, sliced thin

¼ cup cinnamon sugar

Filling

2 lb. cream cheese

½ cup Vermont maple syrup

1 whole egg

¼ cup all-purpose flour

Utensils:

Large bowl

Two 10 inch pie pans, greased and floured

Preparation time: 35 minutes

Oven temp: 375°F

Baking time: About 40 minutes

Results: 2 large tarts

Instructions:

1. **Start with the crust, mixing the butter and brown sugar together until slightly creamy. Add egg and flours. Mix into a workable dough.**

2. **Divide dough into two halves, then each half into thirds. Press two thirds into the bottom of each pie shell. Use the remaining third to use as the rims, crimping around edges.**

3. **Make the filling by combining the cream cheese and maple syrup and beating until creamy. Add the egg and the flour and mix until smooth.**

4. **Spread half the filling into each 10 inch pie shell. Layer the apples over the filling, sprinkle with cinnamon sugar, and brush with maple syrup.**

5. **Preheat oven to 375°F and bake tarts for 40 minutes or until golden. Remove tarts from pans while still slightly warm and chill.**

6. **Serve cool with ice cream or whipped cream.**

Make fresh whipped cream by combining 2 cups heavy cream, ½ cup granulated sugar, and 1 tsp. vanilla. Whip until fluffy.

Happy To Be Picked Second

I had worked in quite a few restaurants in Stowe before I came to the von Trapp Family Lodge. The Trapps would occasionally eat where I was working.

In fact, my first introduction to Maria von Trapp happened when I was cooking at the Spruce Pond Inn – in those days one of Stowe's finest restaurants. Maria, who wasn't shy about anything, walked into the kitchen and tried to hire me right in front of my boss! I was embarrassed too, and having been put on the spot, I said "no."

After awhile, it seemed like the Trapps were eating in my dining room just about every Saturday night. And later on, after I had been working in a couple of other kitchens, Johannes asked me privately if I would come to work at Trapps as the chef.

It turned out that there were two of us who were being considered for the job. A chef named Yvon Roberts was also vying for the position and it turned out that Johannes had already made him an offer. But Johannes didn't want to lose either of us, so he asked me if I would take the pastry chef and baking job if Yvon accepted the chef's job. Well, I'd been lead chef for a lot of years, so being pastry chef would have been a change of vocation and I told Johannes I would think about it.

But all the way back to culinary school, my first love has been pastry cooking and baking. So secretly I was more than happy that Yvon became the chef and I got to be the pastry chef!

Twenty-seven years later, Yvon is still at Trapps and is now the food and beverage director. And I am still there as pastry chef. So Johannes must have had a talent for picking the right people!

Tart and Tangy Key Lime Pie

Ingredients:

Crust
2 cups all-purpose flour
1 cup whole wheat flour
2 cups vegetable shortening
2 tsp. brown sugar
1 cup ice water

Filling
1 lb. cream cheese
3 twelve oz. cans condensed milk
½ cup lemon juice
½ cup lime juice
3 tsp. vanilla
1 drop green food coloring

Utensils:

Large bowl
Floured board
Rolling pin
Two 9 inch pie pans, greased

Preparation time: 35 minutes
Oven temp: 375°F
Baking time: About 20 minutes for the crust only
Results: 2 pies

Instructions:

1. Start with the crust, mixing the flour and shortening together until crumbly. Do not overmix!

2. Add cold water and sugar. Mix just enough to make a smooth dough.

3. Divide dough and roll out two open crusts, ⅛ inch thick. Put in pie pans and crimp edges and bake inverted between 2 pie plates for 20 minutes at 375°F. Add weight to the top of the pans if using metal pans. Not needed for glass pans.

4. Start mixing the filling by combining the cream cheese and condensed milk together slowly until smooth. Add the remaining ingredients and pour equal amounts into each pie shell. Place in refrigerator and allow filling to set.

5. Serve chilled and top with whipped cream.

Make fresh whipped cream by combining 2 cups heavy cream, ½ cup granulated sugar, and 1 tsp. vanilla. Whip until fluffy.

Marshall's Vermont Maple Cream Pie

Ingredients:

Crust
1 cup shortening
1 1/2 cups all-purpose flour
1/2 cup ice water
1/2 tsp. salt

Filling
3 eggs
2 cups Vermont maple syrup
1 cup heavy cream
3 Tbsp. flour, sifted

Utensils:
Two large bowls
Mixing spoon
Wire whisk
9 inch pie pan or
   fluted tart pan

Preparation: 15 minutes
Oven temp: 375°F
Baking time: 30 minutes
Results: One pie, serving eight

Instructions:

1. **Cut the shortening and flour together in the large bowl until it is crumbly. Add the ice water and salt and work it into a dough. Do not overmix.**

2. **Roll out the dough to 1/8 inch thickness and form the shell in pie or tart pan.**

3. **Break the eggs into a bowl and whisk slightly. Add maple syrup, cream, and flour and whisk again for a minute.**

4. **Pour the mixture into the shell and bake at 375°F for 30 minutes. The pie should puff up and be a golden color. The filling will settle as it cools.**

Serve cool with a dollop of whipped cream or a wedge of Vermont cheddar cheese.

Vermont Maple Walnut Cake

Ingredients:

1 cup wheat flour.

1 cup all-purpose flour

1 tsp. salt

2 tsp. baking soda

4 tsp. vanilla

2 tsp. vinegar

$2/3$ cup vegetable oil

1 ½ cups Vermont maple syrup

1 ½ cups buttermilk

1 cup coarsely chopped walnuts

Utensils:

Large bowl

Flour sifter

Two 8 inch cake pans
   greased and floured

Preparation time: 20 minutes

Oven temp: 350°F

Baking time: 20 - 25 minutes or
   until springy to touch

Results: 2 single-layer cakes

Instructions:

1. Place all ingredients in a large bowl.

2. Mix well and put the batter into two greased and floured 8 inch pans.

3. Preheat oven to 350°F and bake for about 20 - 25 minutes or until cakes are springy to the touch.

4. Serve with maple syrup and vanilla ice cream.

Tortes

Now *That's* A Linzertorte!

Maria liked most sweets, especially apple strudel. Her favorite pastry by far was Linzertorte.

When I first started at the Lodge, she didn't like the Linzertorte that I made. She said it was good, but not as good as she remembered it from when she was growing up in Austria.

So over a period of months, I went upstairs to her apartment many times with different recipes for Linzertorte, trying to find one that she liked. And every time, she would say, "This is good, but it isn't *quite* right."

One day Johannes was talking to me and said that in the region of Austria where Maria grew up there were a lot of currants grown. He thought that maybe I should try some red currant in my Linzertorte. So that day I was making Linzertorte and instead of just using straight raspberry jam, I mixed red currant jelly in with it.

Maria tasted it and said, "Now *that's* a Linzertorte!"

And so from that day to this, our Linzertorte is one of the only Linzertortes in the world that is made with raspberry jam and red currant jelly to give it a sweet-tart taste.

Marshall's World Famous Linzertorte

Ingredients:
1 ½ cups granulated sugar
¾ pound butter *(cool)*
1 whole egg
1 ½ cups ground walnuts
3 rounded cups all-purpose flour
½ tsp. cinnamon
½ tsp. nutmeg
¼ tsp. cloves
¼ tsp. salt
¼ cup sliced almonds
¾ cup each currant jelly and raspberry jam

Utensils:
Large bowl
Two 8 inch pans,
   greased and floured
Rolling pin and board

Preparation Time: 20 minutes
Oven temp: 375°F
Baking time: 35 minutes until golden brown
Results: 2 tortes. Each serves 8

Instructions:
1. In a large bowl, cream butter and sugar, add egg, walnuts, all-purpose flour, and spices. Work into dough.
2. Divide dough into quarters.
3. Press one of the quarters into the bottom of each greased and floured 8 inch pan.
4. Roll remaining dough and cut into ½ inch strips. Use some of the strips to line the sides of the pans, pressing the dough into the pan sides. Set aside the remaining strips.
5. Mix the currant jelly and the raspberry jam into a filling and spread it evenly in each pan.
6. Place or weave the remaining strips on top of the filling and sprinkle with the sliced almonds.
7. Preheat oven to 375°F and bake until golden brown and the jam mixture bubbles – approximately 35 minutes.
8. Remove from the oven, cool, and take out of the pans.
9. Just before serving, sprinkle with confectioner's sugar.

Linzertorte keeps without refrigeration in a tight container and it freezes well.

Our Mailorder House

When we first moved to Stowe, we were living in a trailer and saving everything we could to buy a house.

Finally, we were able to buy a couple of acres of land in Nebraska Valley from Gramp Walker, who was parceling his dairy farm. But after buying the land, we certainly couldn't afford to hire a contractor to build a house!

Many years ago it was common for people in rural areas to order a house from a catalog and have it shipped to them as a kit. Sears Roebuck even sold houses by mailorder, offering everything from tiny cabins to huge Victorians. So we ordered a Plant-Griffith low-cost house kit from a cata-

log. A couple of weeks later, a truck arrived and unloaded tons of building materials that we would have to assemble into something resembling a ranch house.

All that summer, when I finished up at the Spruce Pond Inn, Bonnie and I would come down at night. Most of the time, we were pounding nails and putting up sections by Coleman lantern light. We finished just in time for winter.

Later, an architect friend used to come over pretty regularly. He constantly ribbed me about the place, saying, "Marshall, your house has no class." He was right; it was just a straight, simple ranch. So he decided that I needed to put on an addition and one day he showed up with plans he had drawn up. He felt we needed a sunken living room with a vaulted ceiling, a sun room, and a new master bedroom.

Well, there was no stopping him. He was determined to put an addition on our house. So we ordered materials and he brought his family over to help build it. Over a few weekends, both our families – including our combined seven kids – built the addition on the house. Because I don't like heights, the kids did all the climbing to put up the rafters for the vaulted ceilings. He never charged us a dime for all that work.

Our Mailorder House – Continued

In these days of prefab houses and modular construction, I don't know whether you can still order a house from a kit – aside from log cabin kits. But building your own house is an experience. It's not like walking into a house and writing a check. My whole family built this place with their own hands and I know exactly how it all went together.

I am very comfortable here and it's not a place I would easily want to leave.

Lemon Frangipan Torte

Ingredients:

Lemon Sugar Cookie Crust

2 cups *(4 sticks)* butter or margarine at room temperature

1 ¼ cups granulated sugar

3 egg yolks

4 ¼ cups all-purpose flour

1 tsp. lemon zest

¼ tsp. baking powder

Lemon Filling

2 cups any good brand lemon pie filling

Juice of one lemon

Frangipan Cream Filling

1 cup butter or margarine *(room temperature)*

1 ¼ cups granulated sugar

1 cup almond paste

5 whole eggs

¾ cups all-purpose flour

Lemon icing

1 ½ cups sifted confectioners sugar

1 drop lemon yellow color

½ tsp. lemon zest

1 Tbsp. hot water

¼ cup lemon juice

Utensils:

Large bowl/small bowl

Two 8 inch pie pans, greased and floured

Rolling pin and board

Small saucepan

Preparation Time: 35 minutes

Oven temp: 375°F

Baking time: 45 minutes until golden

Results: 2 large tortes, each serves 8 -10

Instructions:

1. **Begin by making the sugar crust dough. In a large bowl mix the sugar and the butter slightly. Add flour, egg, and baking powder. Work into a smooth dough, keeping the dough cool.**

2. **Divide dough in half and divide one of the halves in half again. Line the bottom and sides of pie pans with dough and**

Lemon Frangipan Torte Instructions – Continued on page 79.

set aside as 2 shells. *(Freeze the leftover half or use for sugar cookies.)*

3. Mix 2 cups lemon filling *(made as per package directions)* and the juice of one lemon and set aside.

4. Work almond paste and sugar together by rubbing until they are well blended; add butter and work together until dough is smooth. Add eggs, one at a time, and blend in well. Fold flour into the mix. Set aside.

5. Place 1 cup lemon filling in each shell, spreading out the filling evenly. Place 2 ½ cups frangipan cream over the lemon filling of each torte and smooth out. It should come almost to the top of each shell.

6. Preheat oven to 375°F and bake tortes for approximately 45 minutes until the filling is set and golden in color. It will rise up slightly and settle when it cools.

7. When cool, place sugar and lemon juice in a stainless steel or glass bowl. Add hot water, zest, and color. Stir to a smooth icing. *(If it is too thin, add more sugar; if it is too thick, add more water.)* Drip icing on the tortes.

"You Must Be My Most Reliable Employee!"

When I first started at Trapps, there was a gas shortage and I had an old 350 Honda Scrambler motorcycle. It was pretty loud because it didn't have any mufflers, but living way out in the country I didn't think I was bothering anyone.

I'd get up in the morning and get it kick started at about 3:30 so I could get to work at 4:00 sharp. I'd ride out Nebraska Valley, run through the gears as I climbed Trapp Hill Road, and get up enough speed at the top so I could shut off the motor and coast into the lodge without disturbing the guests.

After I had been doing that for a few months, Johannes Von Trapp, the lodge manager, came to see me.

He said, "Marshall, you must be my most reliable employee. I can hear you start that motorcycle on the other side of the valley every single morning at 3:30. I can hear you run through every gear on your way up the valley every single morning at 3:45. And when you're gunning your motor halfway up the hill to get enough speed to coast to the lodge, you are right next to my house! So I appreciate your punctuality, but either get a set of mufflers or find some other way to get to work!"

I bought a set of new mufflers that day.

Nut Streusel Sour Cream Torte

Ingredients:

Cake
½ cup butter *(1 stick)*
2 cups granulated sugar
2 tsp. vanilla
½ tsp. salt
4 eggs
2 cups sour cream
4 cups all-purpose flour
2 tsp. baking powder
2 tsp. baking soda

Topping
1 ¼ cup chopped pecans
1 cup granulated sugar
3 tsp. cinnamon

Utensils:
Two large bowls
Two 8 inch bundt or tube
   pans, greased and floured
Rolling pin and board

Preparation Time: 30 minutes
Oven temp: 350°F
Baking time: 40 minutes
Results: 2 tortes, each serves 6 - 8

Instructions:

1. Begin by mixing the nuts, sugar, and cinnamon and set aside.

2. Next make the batter. Start by combining the butter and sugar, beating until creamy. Add eggs, vanilla, and sour cream. Mix well, then add flour, baking powder, baking soda, and salt. Mix thoroughly.

3. Divide *HALF* the batter evenly between two greased and floured bundt pans. Divide *HALF* nut mixture evenly and put on top of the batter in each pan. Pour the remaining batter evenly on top of each pan. Then top each pan evenly with the remaining nut mixture.

4. Preheat oven to 350°F and bake tortes for 40 minutes until springy to the touch.

5. Cool tortes and serve.

Nut Streusel Sour Cream Torte keeps without refrigeration in a tight container and it freezes well.

The Things We Do For Our Guests

The winter of 1976 or 1977 was one of those classic New England winters where we measured the snow in feet, not inches. That year we had snow every day, all winter. It never quit.

We finally had a monster snow storm of about 30 inches. The plows were all off the road and stuck; trees were down everywhere, along with power and phones. Nothing was moving. Not many people had four-wheel-drives back then and even my chainsaw-equipped old grey Willys Jeep truck wasn't up to handling that much snow.

But Trapps had a full house of guests who were snowed in and getting hungry!

The other chef and kitchen staffers lived across town, but I live in Nebraska Valley. By road, I am about five miles from the lodge. But by snowshoe, through the woods, it's just a couple of miles so I figured I had to get into work.

I put on my wool hunting clothes and bundled up well. I strapped on my snowshoes and headed up through the woods to Trapps through almost five feet of accumulated powder snow.

That morning I was not only the baker, I was breakfast cook, waiter, and dishwasher for our snowbound – and grateful – guests.

Poppy Seed Torte

Ingredients:

1 ½ cups *(3 sticks)* butter
1 tsp. vanilla
2 cups all-purpose flour
¼ tsp. salt
¾ cups poppy seeds
3 cups granulated sugar
3 whole eggs
1 ½ tsp. baking powder
1 ½ cups sour cream

Utensils:

Large bowl
Two 8-inch spring
  form pie pans,
  greased and floured

Preparation Time: 20 minutes
Oven temp: 350°F
Baking time: 30 minutes until golden
Results: Two 8 inch tortes
  Each serves 6 - 8

Instructions:

1. In a large bowl, beat the butter and sugar thoroughly until creamy. Add vanilla and eggs.

2. Add flour, baking powder, and salt. Mix thoroughly until creamy. Fold in sour cream and poppy seeds, mixing thoroughly.

3. Pour batter equally into two 8 inch spring form pie pans that have been greased and floured.

4. Preheat oven to 350°F and bake cakes for about 30 minutes until golden and firm to the touch.

5. Serve warm or cool. If desired, drizzle with lemon glaze *(see Lemon Rings recipe page 101)* or with whipped cream.

Poppy Seed Torte keeps without refrigeration in a tight container and it freezes well.

Workin' In A Coal Mine

Most people think of a pastry kitchen and picture something out of Julia Child or The Galloping Gourmet. Pastry kitchens are spotless white rooms with rows of stainless pans and high-tech mixing tools, right?

Not so when I started working at the von Trapp Family Lodge.

The first bake shop was built in the lodge coal bin!

The coal bin dated to the early days of the lodge – when they were still heating with coal. The coal bin was in the basement, up against an outside wall. Opposite the bin were the furnaces. All winter long dump trucks would back up to a huge chute and empty tons of coal into the bins. The coal was then shoveled into the old furnaces.

By the time I started working for the Trapp family, the lodge was heated with oil and the coal bins weren't being used. So the bins were emptied and cleaned up. They moved in an oven and mixer and the coal bin became my baking and pastry kitchen.

I didn't have a window, but I could peek outside through the vent fan! Today we have a modern, beautiful kitchen under the Austrian Tea Room.

And I have four huge windows!

Of course, they offered to cover them with plywood if it would have made me more comfortable.

Sachertorte *(Sugar Torte)*

Ingredients:

Crust
1 cup *(2 sticks)* butter
1 ¾ cups granulated sugar
6 whole eggs
2 tsp. vanilla
1 ¼ cups all-purpose flour
⅔ cups powdered cocoa
1 tsp. baking powder
¼ cup whole milk
⅓ cup ground almonds

Filling
2 cups apricot preserves

Glaze
2 cups heavy cream
2 cups *(heaped)* chopped
   dark chocolate

Utensils:
Two large bowls
Two 8 inch pie pans, greased and
   floured
Rolling pin and board
Small saucepan
Sharp knife at least 12 inches long

Preparation Time: 35 minutes
Oven temp: 325°F
Baking time: 40 minutes until
   springy
Results: Two large tortes, each
   serving 6 - 8

Instructions:
1. Begin by making the crust. In a large bowl mix the sugar and the butter until light and creamy. Add the eggs and vanilla and mix until smooth.

2. In a separate bowl, sift cocoa, flour, and baking powder together, mixing thoroughly.

3. Add half the flour to the egg mix and mix until smooth. Add half the milk and mix until smooth. Add remaining flour and remaining milk and mix until smooth. Then fold in the almonds.

4. Pour batter into two greased and floured pie pans. Preheat oven to 325°F and bake for about 40 minutes until cakes are springy to the touch. Cool for 15 - 20 minutes and remove from pans, then chill.

5. While cakes are chilling, make glaze. In a small saucepan scald heavy cream. Reduce heat, add chocolate, and allow to melt, stirring constantly until smooth. Cool to room temperature or pouring consistency.

6. Remove cakes from refrigerator and using a long knife, carefully split each one into thirds *(three layers)*. Spread ½ cup apricot preserves on the bottom and middle layer and stack. Pour chocolate glaze over torte and chill.

Serve with whipped cream and decorate with shaved dark chocolate.

Maria's Sweet Tooth

Back when we were in the old lodge, I would always get a pot of coffee brewing in the bakery first thing in the morning when I

arrived. And by 4:30 or 5:00 in the morning, the first pastries were coming out of the oven. So the place was always pretty inviting.

For years Maria von Trapp used to get up very early in the morning and come down to the bakery. She liked her coffee very sweet and would have two cups of coffee and whatever I had coming out of the oven as her breakfast.

Later on, Maria had a nurse/dietitian who lived with her in her suite of rooms in the lodge. The nurse immediately declared my bakery – and all its contents – off limits. Maria found herself on a breakfast diet of tea, dry toast, and a poached egg, which was not to her liking at all.

But Maria quickly discovered that her nurse liked to sleep late in the morning. Maria, on the other hand, was still an early riser. So she would come down to the bakery about 5:00 in the morning and have a pastry or two hot from the oven, along with

her usual sweet coffee. Then she would go back to bed and the nurse would wake her up and accompany her to the lodge where she would have her "healthy" breakfast.

She swore me to secrecy and I knew my job was at stake if I said anything.

Salzberg Lemon Torte

Ingredients:

Sugar Crust

1 ¼ cups soft margarine
Grated peel of two lemons
1 cup granulated sugar
4 whole eggs, beaten
3 ½ cups all-purpose flour
1 cup corn starch
1 ½ tsp. baking powder
2 cups whole milk

Syrup

6 Tbsp. water
2 Tbsp. lemon juice
2 Tbsp. Arak, Ouzo or Sambuca
6 Tbsp. granulated sugar

Icing

4 cups sifted confectioners sugar
6 Tbsp. lemon juice
2 drops yellow food coloring *(optional)*

Utensils:

Two large bowls
Two 8 inch pie pans,
   greased and floured
Rolling pin and board
Small saucepan
Whisk

Preparation Time: 35 minutes

Oven temp: 375°F

Baking time: 30 minutes until springy to
   the touch.

Results: 2 eight inch round tortes,
   each serving 6 - 8

Instructions:

1. Begin by making the crust pastry. In a large bowl beat the margarine, lemon peel, and sugar until light and creamy. Stir in eggs and milk.

2. In a separate bowl, dry mix flour, cornstarch, and baking powder. Sift into the liquid and work into a smooth dough.

3. Put equal amounts of dough into the two 8 inch pie pans.

4. Preheat oven to 375°F. Bake for about 30 minutes until springy to the touch.

5. While baking, make the syrup. In a small saucepan, boil the water, lemon juice, and sugar, adding the liqueur when the mixture comes to a boil. Remove from heat immediately and let cool slightly.

6. As soon as cakes are removed from the oven, brush syrup on, soaking them.

7. Mix icing ingredients together and whisk until smooth. Spread or drizzle evenly over the cakes.

8. Cool cakes and serve.

Salzberg Lemon Torte keeps without refrigeration in a tight container and it freezes well.

The Ghost Of Trapp Hill Road

Driving up Trapp Hill Road to work early in the morning, I have seen every animal native to the Vermont woods. I've also seen a few strange things!

The strangest thing occurred one morning as I was driving my old gray Willys Jeep truck up Trapp Hill Road. That old Jeep didn't go very fast, especially up the steep hill. But that was a good thing that particular day because there was a thick fog and it was rainy and I had to concentrate to keep from driving off the road.

Just as I reached Johannes and Lynn von Trapp's house – about halfway up the hill – I saw this apparition float across the road in front of me and disappear! I'd been hunting and in the outdoors all my life and I'd never seen anything like that.

I blinked and stopped the Jeep, got out and started to look around. I looked all around and didn't find anything. And the whole time I'm saying to myself, "I saw something! I know I saw something." Well, I didn't find anything and I didn't dare tell anybody. They would figure I'd gone over the edge!

After a few weeks, I had mostly forgotten about the apparition. But one day I was talking to Lynn von Trapp and being the modest person that she is, she asked me if I had seen her in her nightgown.

I didn't know what to say, but she went on to solve the mystery. Lynn told me that she had gone out early in the morning to check on her horses in the barn across the road from the house. She was wearing a pair of black rubber boots and a long, flowing white night-ie. Just as she was crossing the road, my Jeep crested the hill and the headlights caught her full on through the fog.

She didn't want anyone to see her in nightclothes, so she ran across the road and hid behind the barn where I couldn't see her.

I was some relieved to find out that it wasn't a ghost I had seen!

Winter Apricot Torte

Ingredients:

Sugar Crust

1 cup granulated sugar
2 cups *(4 sticks)* butter, room temperature
1 whole egg
½ tsp. baking powder
Apricot halves, drained
6 oz. jar apricot preserves for glaze
¼ cup whole almonds for decoration

Filling

¾ cup heavy cream
¾ cup sugar
3 whole eggs
1 cup ground
   almonds

Utensils:

Large bowl
Two 10 inch pie pans,
   greased and floured
Rolling pin and board
Small saucepan

Preparation Time: 35 minutes

Oven temp: 375°F
Baking time: 45 minutes until golden.
Results: 2 large tortes, each
   serves 8 - 10

Instructions:

1. Begin by making the sugar crust dough. In a large bowl mix the sugar and the butter slightly. Add flour, egg, and baking powder. Work into a smooth dough, keeping the dough cool.

2. Divide dough in half and divide one of the halves in half again. Line the bottom and sides of pie pans with dough and set aside. *(Use the leftover half of the dough to make sugar cookies or freeze.)*

3. Make filling by mixing all ingredients, beating until smooth. Divide filling and spread half in each crust. Place apricot halves, center up, filling crust.

4. Garnish the center of each apricot half with an almond.

5. Preheat oven to 375°F and bake tortes approximately 45 minutes until golden. Cool.

6. When torte is cool, warm apricot preserves in a small sauce pan. Bring to boil and remove from heat immediately. Brush hot preserves on each torte.

7. Cool and serve with whipped cream or ice cream.

Apricot torte keeps without refrigeration in a tight container and it freezes well.

Desserts

Praying For A Cuppa

The von Trapp's are a very religious family with strong ties to the church. In fact, there are small shrines around the property. As a result, the lodge often has guests who are there on a retreat or who get up each morning to go out to one of the shrines to say their prayers at sunrise or to enjoy the view of the valley.

One morning I was driving my old grey Jeep into the bakery before sunrise. I got to the top of the hill and kneeling beside the road was a very elderly lady with her hands in a praying position and her head bowed.

I drove slowly by her and for some reason I got worried. Nobody else was out there and while I saw a lot of people who visited the nearby shrine, I wasn't used to seeing people out praying right by the roadside. So I stopped and got out of the Jeep and walked back to where she was kneeling.

I walked up to her, kind of worried that I would disturb her prayers. "Excuse me ma'am," I said. "Are you all right? Is there anything I can do for you?"

She looked up at me and said, "Yes, you can help me take the top off this *damn* Thermos bottle!"

She wasn't praying at all. She wanted her tea while she watched the sunrise over the mountain!

Austrian Apfelstrudel

Ingredients:
4 sheets filo dough from your grocery store
¾ cup *(1 ½ sticks)* melted butter
½ cup bread crumbs
½ cup thin sliced almonds
2 cups sliced fresh Vermont apples
½ cup raisins *(mixed dark and golden optional)*
½ tsp. cinnamon
⅛ tsp. nutmeg
Pinch ginger
¼ cup granulated sugar
1 egg, beaten

Utensils:
Flour sifter
One baking pan,
  greased and floured

Preparation time: 35 minutes
Oven temp: 400°F
Baking time: 30 - 40 minutes or
  until golden brown
Results: 1 strudel or five servings

Instructions:
1. Lay out two layers of filo dough on a damp cloth. Sprinkle with melted butter and half of the bread crumbs.

2. Top with two more layers of filo dough and repeat with the melted butter and crumbs. Arrange the apple slices, raisins, and almonds on the dough.

3. Mix cinnamon, nutmeg, ginger, and granulated sugar into a small bowl and sprinkle liberally on top of the filling. Roll up the strudel.

4. Transfer to baking pan and brush with beaten egg, then brush with melted butter.

5. Preheat oven to 400°F and bake strudel for about 30 - 40 minutes until golden brown.

6. Serve warm from the oven with a scoop of ice cream.

We Were All Part Of
The von Trapp Family

In cooking, it's rare to spend 25 years working in one place. Yet many of us have worked at the von Trapp Family Lodge for years and years. I attribute that to the fact that the von Trapps always treated the staff at the lodge as part of the family.

Maria von Trapp always asked that she be called Mother Trapp. Not Maria. Not Mrs. von Trapp. Always Mother Trapp.

Every Christmas, a huge tree went up for the staff and there were presents for each one of us from Maria. She would send her personal assistant out before Christmas to find out what people would like and she would go to great lengths to fill our Christmas wishes.

That was pretty neat and it made you feel a part of the family. Whether you were a dishwasher or the head chef, you were part of the von Trapp Family.

From left to right: Ken Kaplan, Maria (Maria von Trapp's daughter),
and Marshall as Santa.
Photo of filming for "Good Morning America"

Fresh Fruit Flan

Ingredients:

Almond Murbteig Crust
1/2 cup granulated sugar
1 cup *(2 sticks)* butter
2 1/4 cups all-purpose flour
1/2 whole egg
1/4 tsp. baking powder
1/2 cup ground almonds
Fresh seasonal fruit, sliced thin

Filling
1 cup cream cheese
1 tsp. almond extract
1/4 cup confectioners
sugar

Glaze
1 cup apricot, orange or
clear jelly

Utensils:
Large bowl
Small saucepan
Fine sieve
Two buttered 9 inch pie pans

Preparation time: 35 minutes
Oven Temp: 175°F
Baking Time: 20 minutes
Results: 2 flans

Instructions:

1. Mix sugar and butter, beating until slightly creamy. Add remaining crust ingredients, except the fresh fruit. Work into a smooth dough, keeping the dough cool.

2. Divide the dough in half and then divide each half into thirds. Press two thirds into the bottom of each pie pan and use the remaining third to make the sides. Bake at 175°F for 20 minutes, then set aside to cool.

3. In a separate bowl, combine the filling ingredients and work into a smooth paste. Spread into the shell, covering the bottom only. Add fruit slices to cover the filling.

4. Make a glaze by warming 1 cup jelly on stove on low heat in a small saucepan until smooth. Work it through a sieve and return to saucepan. Bring to boil, remove immediately from heat, and brush on fruit to finish the pastry.

5. Chill flan and serve in pie slices.

What Goes "WOOF!" And Eats Apples?

Like bakers and pastry chefs everywhere, I usually get into work before sunrise.

Most days, the security guard would turn on the light outside my bakery. That made it easy for me to take my usual shortcut in from the parking lot: hop the stone wall, cut across the apple orchard, and walk through the back yard to get to the bakery door.

Some mornings, though, the guard would forget to turn on the light or I'd be a little early. So I got pretty skilled at navigating the shortcut obstacle course in the dark.

One crisp fall morning, I got into work and the guard hadn't turned the light on yet. So I walked through the parking lot and jumped the low stone wall. As soon as my feet hit the ground, I heard a rustle and a "WOOF" right next to me.

My first thought was, "Oh man. What goes "WOOF!" and eats apples?" *A bear of course!*

Just at that moment, the night watchman turned the light on and I was nose to nose with a black bear that was under a tree eating apples! I don't know which one of us was more scared, but the bear went running one way and I went running toward the lodge.

To make matters worse, the guard had looked out the door and seen the bear. And he was so scared that he locked the back door! He wouldn't let me in!

Fortunately, the bear was long gone.

Trapp Family Lodge Babka

Ingredients:

1 cup warm milk
2 tsp. sugar
2 Tbsp. Saf-instant yeast
6 cups unbleached flour
6 eggs
1 tsp. salt
½ cup butter (1 stick)
½ cup sugar
½ cup currants & raisins mixxed
1 tsp. orange zest
1 tsp. lemon zest
¼ tsp. cardamun

Rum Syrup:

1 cup water
1 cup granulated sugar
2 Tbsp. Rum

Water Icing:

2 cups confectioners sugar
½ cup water

Utensils:

Large bowl
Two bread pans,
   greased and floured

Preparation time: 45 minutes

Oven temp: 350°F
Baking time: About 30 - 40 minutes
Results: 2 Babkas

Instructions:

1. Place all ingredients in large bowl with warm milk added last.

2. Rise to double – knock back down and form 2 pans. Rise again to double.

3. Preheat oven to 350° and bake for 30 - 40 minutes.

4. While warm, prick the surface and brush with rum syrup.

5. May be iced with water icing when cold.

Cookies And Crackers

The Most Horrible Night That Anyone Can Remember

Not much has been said about the fire which destroyed the lodge in 1980. But without the fire, I don't think we would have the resort we have today.

The fire happened just before Christmas. It was one of those cold, below zero New England nights. It was also snowing hard that night and there was already a lot of snow on the ground.

The fire started at night in the lodge, which was made mostly of logs and had wooden floors, walls and roof. The fire leapt through the lodge in minutes. The flames got so big that the light woke people up ten miles away in Stowe Hollow. My copper pots melted. The next day, the smoke and burning smell hung over the whole town.

Volunteer firefighters brought their equipment from Stowe, Waterbury, Morrisville and as far away as Hardwick and Johnson. But in the cold, water spilling off the trucks as they navigated the steep hill caused the roads to ice up, so one of the fire trucks skidded off the road into the ditch and got stuck.

The firefighters did all they could that night, but the fire was just too much for anyone to handle. A huge lodge made entirely of wood – fully in flames – is no match for hoses. But the firefighters never gave up. They were all heroes that night.

Fortunately, nobody was hurt. But the loss was hard for all of us.

I not only had all my recipes and records in the bakery, but I had hidden all my family's Christmas presents in my locker to keep my kids from finding them. So there we were, days before Christmas, with no idea if I still had a job. And no presents for our four kids.

In the following weeks, there were actually times when we had some doubts about whether they would rebuild. But Johannes is a dreamer and had a vision. The family worked hard to build the new lodge from the ashes – newer, bigger, better.

In the year before the new lodge opened, we kept the dining room and the tea room open. We leased a bakery in the village from 5 PM to 5 AM – so for more than a year I worked all night. That was rough.

But no matter how bad it got, the von Trapps found a way to make sure the staff got paid. We never missed a paycheck. We respected them a lot for that.

Almond Cookies

Ingredients:

1 ½ rounded cups granulated sugar
¾ cup butter *(1 ½ sticks)*
¾ cup vegetable oil
1 whole egg
½ tsp. almond extract
3 ¾ cups all-purpose flour
¼ tsp. baking soda
¼ tsp. salt
1 egg white, beaten, to brush on top of cookies
Blanched whole almonds for top of each cookie

Utensils:

Large bowl
Two large, greased
 cookie sheets

Preparation Time: 25 minutes
Oven Temp: 375°F
Baking Time: 10 minutes
Results: 2 dozen cookies

Instructions:

1. **Mix the sugar, butter, and oil and beat until creamy.**
2. **Add remaining ingredients, except whole almonds and egg white; mix into a light dough.**
3. **Roll dough into 1 inch balls and place on greased cookie sheets.**
4. **Press a whole almond into each ball and brush each with beaten egg white.**
5. **Preheat oven to 375°F. Bake cookies for about 10 minutes until golden. Cool and serve.**

Store Almond Cookies in a tight container or freeze.

Raising 46 Children

In 1980 my wife Bonnie and I were raising our two kids, Josh and Tori. We decided to take a state-run parenting class because we thought we would like to be better parents for our kids and because the state was paying parents to attend. In those days, we were always looking for ways to get a little extra cash.

Bonnie and I had been in the class for a couple of weeks when we were approached by someone from the state who said, "We'd like to intro-

duce you to foster care. Would you be interested in becoming foster parents and taking in a little girl who desperately needs a home." We thought about it and figured we have our own two, so one more wouldn't be too bad.

The next night I got home from work and Bonnie told me that the state had called and explained that the girl had a brother who was 12 and he needed a home too. She said the state was going to separate them unless we could take both. I thought about it and said, "Well, I never had a brother. But if I did, I would hate to be separated. So let's take both of them."

And overnight, we went from a family of four to a family of six. And in the past 21 years, we have been foster parents to 44 neglected and abused children. We have seen several through college; and two are serving in the armed forces. Many of them are still as much a part of my family as Josh and Tori.

The two kids who joined us in 1981? John is now a tank driver in the United States Army and has served his country in the U.S. and overseas for nearly ten years. And Angela, the little girl who started it all, went on to college and earned her degree. And she is now a mother herself. She and her husband have a beautiful baby girl and I am the world's proudest foster grandparent!

Though making a difference in the lives of all those kids was reward enough, over the years we were also proud to have been named Lamoille County Foster Parents of the Year; Burlington District Foster Parents of the Year; Easter Seals Foster Parents of the Year; and Vermont State Foster Parents of the Year.

I only wish Bonnie, who passed on just a few weeks before the baby was born, had lived to see Angie's little daughter.

Orange Biscuits

Ingredients:

4 cups all-purpose flour

1 ½ tsp. salt

2 Tbsp. baking powder

¾ cup butter *(1 ½ sticks)*

4 Tbsp. brown sugar

1 ¾ cup milk *(cold)*

Egg Wash

1 beaten egg

Orange Filling

¼ cup concentrated orange juice

1 ½ cup granulated sugar

Utensils:
Large bowl
Floured board
Two cookie sheets

Preparation Time: 20 minutes
Oven Temp: 375°F
Baking Time: 20 minutes approximately
Results: 2 dozen biscuits

Instructions:

1. **Cut butter and dry ingredients together**
2. **Add milk and mix lightly to dough**
3. **Pat out on floured board and cut into shapes. Brush with beaten egg and press a thumb print into each center.**
4. **Mix orange filling to paste and fill in thumb print in each biscuit.**
5. **Bake at 375°F for approximately 20 minutes.**

Cranberry White Chocolate Chip Cookies

Ingredients:

½ pound soft butter *(2 sticks)*
1 cup packed light brown sugar
¾ cup granulated sugar
1 tsp. salt
2 tsp. vanilla
½ tsp. orange zest
1 egg
½ tsp. baking soda
2 ¾ cups all-purpose flour
1 ½ cups white chocolate chips
1 ½ cups dried cranberries
1 cup chopped walnuts

Utensils:

Large bowl
Two greased cookie
  sheets

Preparation time: 17 minutes
Oven temp: 375°F
Baking time: About 14 - 17 minutes
Results: 4 dozen

Instructions:

1. **Place all ingredients into large bowl**

2. **Mix well and scoop onto two greased cookies sheets. Flatten slightly.**

3. **Bake at 375°F for 14 - 17 minutes.**

Mandel Makronen
(Almond Macaroons)

Ingredients:

4 egg whites
2/3 cup granulated sugar
1 tsp. vanilla extract
4 cups finely ground almonds
Blanched whole almonds – one per cookie

Utensils:

Medium-sized bowl
Lightly buttered cookie
   sheet

Preparation Time: 20 minutes
Oven Temp: 300°F
Baking Time: 18 minutes
Results: 2 dozen macaroons

Instructions:

1. Stir the egg whites, sugar, and vanilla until foamy. Add ground almonds and blend until smooth.

2. Drop teaspoonsfulls of mixture, 2 inches apart, on buttered cookie sheet pan, creating high mounds. Decorate with a whole almond, pressing it slightly into the mixture.

3. Preheat oven to 300°F. Bake macaroons for approximately 18 minutes or until lightly colored and the tips are firmed. Cool and serve.

Store macaroons in a tightly sealed container.

Professor Marshall

Not long after the lodge burned, Johannes made the decision that to help raise funds to rebuild the lodge, we would put in timeshare units. The income would help build the new lodge. That was a risky decision at the time because timeshare units were on the decline and we were worried that we would have a tough time selling units.

To help bring in prospective owners, I got recruited to teach baking classes to people who came to look at buying timeshares. The first class was called the "Pattycake Bake-Off." There were 12 people in the class and ten of them bought timeshare units. Needless to say, I was teaching a lot of baking classes after that!

All our timeshares were quickly sold and I have continued to teach baking classes at Trapps to our timeshare and hotel guests. Many of our guests come back every year for a baking class and say it's the highlight of their vacation in Stowe. My students are also the ones who got me to write my cookbook. Every year, without fail, they would ask me when I was going to write a cookbook that they can take home along with their pastries!

But the best part of teaching is that people who come to classes have become like old friends. The chance to interact with our guests has been one of the best parts of being at the Trapp Family Lodge all these years and I feel a real attachment with a lot of our guests and my former students.

It really hit home when my wife passed on and I received cards and letters and prayers from people all over the country. These people felt a personal friendship with me through the baking classes and folks whom I hadn't seen in years took the time to write a letter or send a card expressing their heartfelt sympathies.

Apparently I had touched more people through teaching than I had ever thought possible.

Amandel Fierkken
(Almond Streusel Squares)

Ingredients:

Sugar Cookie Dough
2 cups *(4 sticks)* butter room temperature
1 1/4 cups granulated sugar
3 egg yolks
4 1/2 cups all-purpose flour
1 cup apricot preserves

Frangipan Cream
1 cup *(2 sticks)* butter or margarine
1 1/4 cup granulated sugar
1 cup almond paste
5 eggs
3/4 cup all-purpose flour

Streussel Topping
2 3/4 cup pastry flour
1/2 cup brown sugar, packed
3/4 cup *(1 1/2 sticks)* butter, room temperature
1 Tbsp. Vermont honey
3/8 cup almond paste
Glaze made of 1/4 cup water and 1 cup confectioners sugar

Final Topping
Cinnamon sugar *(1 cup granulated sugar with 2 Tbsp. cinnamon)*

Utensils:
Three large bowls
Two 8 inch pans and one 8 x 11 inch pan, greased and floured
Coarse sieve

Preparation Time: 45 minutes
Oven Temp: 375°F
Baking Time: 20 minutes
Results: About two dozen squares

Instructions:

1. **For sugar cookie dough, allow the butter to warm up and soften for about 1/2 hour.**
2. **In a large bowl, mix butter, sugar, egg yolks, and flour together to form a workable dough. Press cookie dough into a pan or cookie sheet. Set aside.**
3. **In a second bowl, mix frangipan cream. Start by working almond paste and sugar together until well-blended. Add butter and beat until smooth.**
4. **Add eggs, one at a time, and blend in well. Fold flour into the mix. Blend until smooth.**
5. **Spread apricot preserves and then the frangipan evenly over the dough.**
6. **Mix streusel topping by working all ingredients together into a dough and press it through a very coarse sieve or cooling rack. Dust with flour as you sieve it. Spinkle liberally on top of frangipan cream and dust with cinnamon sugar.**
7. **Preheat oven to 375°F and bake for 20 minutes. Cool, cut into squares.**

Store squares in a tight container or freeze.

Moscow, Vermont Style

Completely surrounded by the town of Stowe is a small village called Moscow. It's a true town with its own post office, gas station, and general store – all in the same building.

For many years, the building was Decelle's Market and Paul Decelle was the "mayor," postmaster, and storekeeper. Now it's the Moscow General Store and is owned by Alex and Sarah Leveille, who grew up next door to the market, bought the store from Paul a few years ago, and still run it. Moscow has one of the last post offices in the U.S. that is still located inside a working general store.

Moscow is also famous for inventing something called "The Boom Box Parade" which takes place every 4th of July. The parade was started by Tom Hamilton who lives right in Moscow. Since the town was too small to have a marching band and we weren't about to import a band from Stowe, Tom convinced our local radio station, WDEV, to play marching music at 10:00. Everyone would come out of their houses with their radios playing marching music for the parade! One year, CBS came out and we were all on national TV marching through Moscow.

There are only two rules for the parade. One is that you can only start working on your float an hour before the parade. No fair staying up the night before, your float has to be completely impromptu. I would often hitch my fishing boat up to my lawn tractor and we'd load all the kids in the boat. I'd get a big fish out of the freezer and put that in a net hanging off the boat. At the end of the parade, we'd give the fish away for someone to take home and grill. One year Bonnie dressed up a pig and walked it down Main Street.

The other rule is that the newest resident of Moscow has to walk at the back of the parade with a wheelbarrow and a shovel to pick up anything left by the horses. It definitely isn't a good idea to move into Moscow in June.

The Moscow parade still takes place every Independence Day and people come from all over New England to watch a Yankee parade at its finest.

Hazelnuss Pfeffernuse

Ingredients:

1 cup semi-sweet chocolate chips

³/₄ cup butter *(1 ¹/₂ sticks)*

1 ¹/₂ cups confectioners sugar

2 ¹/₂ cups finely chopped toasted hazelnuts
(use food processor)

Utensils:
Food processor
Large bowl
#100 cookie scoop
Two cookie sheets

Preparation Time: 10 minutes
Oven Temp: 350°F
Baking Time: 10 minutes approximately
Results: 2 dozen cookies

Instructions:

1. Melt chocolate chips over a water-bath or in a microvave oven and allow to cool.

2. Mix butter and confectioners sugar together.

3. Add chocolate chips and hazelnuts. Mix well.

4. Scoop with #100 cookie scoop or roll into 1 inch rolls and cut into 1 inch pieces

5. Roll round.

6. Place on greased cookies sheets and bake at 350°F for approximately 10 minutes

Old Towne Molasses Cookies

Ingredients:

½ cup butter *(1 stick)*

1 cup molasses

½ cup granulated sugar

½ cup hot water

2 tsp. baking soda

½ tsp. salt

1 tsp. ginger

1 egg

4 cups all-purpose flour

Utensils:

Large bowl

Two cookie sheets

Preparation time: 20 minutes

Oven temp: 350°F

Baking time: About 8 - 10 minutes

Results: 2 - 3 dozen

Instructions:

1. **Cream the sugar, egg and molasses.**

2. **Disolve baking soda in water and add to mixture in large bowl.**

3. **Add remaining ingredients and mix well.**

4. **Scoop or roll out and cut into 1 inch pieces.**

5. **Roll in granulated sugar and place on cookie sheets, pressing down slightly.**

6. **Bake at 350°F for 8 - 10 minutes.**

Chocolate Crackle Cookies

Ingredients:

1 ½ cups all-purpose flour
1 cup granulated sugar
½ cup cocoa powder
2 whole eggs
4 Tbsp. *(1/2 stick)* butter
2 cups bakers snow *(1 cup cornstarch mixed with 1 cup confectioners sugar)*
One chocolate kiss for each cookie

Utensils:
Large bowl
One greased cookie sheet

Preparation Time: 25 minutes
Oven Temp: 350°F
Baking Time: 8 minutes
Results: 2 dozen cookies

Instructions:

1. In a large bowl, mix the flour, sugar, cocoa, eggs, and butter into a soft dough.
2. Scoop, roll into cylindrical shape about the diameter of a quarter, and cut into 1 ounce cookies about 1 inch long.
3. Roll each cookie in bakers snow and place on greased cookie sheet.
4. Preheat oven to 350°F. Bake cookies about 8 minutes until puffed up.
5. Remove from oven and while still hot, press a chocolate kiss into the center of each cookie.
6. Cool and serve.

Store Chocolate Crackle Cookies in a tight container or freeze.

Fruit Pinwheels

Ingredients:
Puff Dough from your local store
  (dough comes in 5 inch squares)
Apricot jam
Apricot glaze

Icing
1/4 cup cold water
1 cup icing sugar

Utensils:
Large bowl
Two large, greased
  cookie sheets

Preparation Time: 10 minutes
Oven Temp: 375°F
Baking Time: 10 minutes
Results: 24 pinwheels

Instructions:
1. Cut from inside out as diagrammed and fold dough corners, *as marked*, into pinwheels. Place apricot jam in center.

2. Preheat oven to 375°F. Bake for about 10 minutes, then remove from the oven. Let pinwheels cool.

3. While cookies are cooling, make water icing by combining water and confectioners sugar and mixing until smooth.

4. Warm apricot preserves to form glaze and brush over pinwheels.

5. Drizzle glazed pinwheels with icing.

Store pinwheels in a tight container or freeze.

Good Ol' Gingersnaps

Ingredients:
1 ½ cups butter *(3 sticks)*
2 cups sugar
2 whole eggs
½ cup molasses
4 cups all-purpose flour
1 tsp. baking soda
2 tsp. salt
4 – 6 tsp. ginger
1 tsp. cinnamon
Confectioners sugar

Utensils:
Large bowl
Greased cookie
   sheet

Preparation Time: 20 minutes
Oven Temp: 350°F
Baking Time: 10 minutes
Results: 2 dozen ginger snaps

Instructions:

1. **Place all ingredients, except confectioner's sugar, into bowl and mix together.**
2. **Scoop or cut dough into nickel-sized balls and roll in confectioners sugar.**
3. **Place on greased pan.**
4. **Preheat oven to 350°F. Bake Cookies for 10 minutes until crisp.**
5. **Cool and serve.**

Store gingersnaps in a tight container or freeze.

"Dad, I Want To Be A Chef"

My son Josh had worked with me in the bakery at von Trapp's during the summers. But he didn't really like the early hours that went along with being a baker. So when Josh came to me and said, "Dad, I want to be a chef," I was pretty surprised.

I said that I would like him to go to the Culinary Institute of America in Hyde Park, New York. I had gone to the CIA when it was in New Haven and felt that if he was going to really succeed as a chef, he should have a first-rate education.

It was a struggle to get him through school. Bonnie and I had not been able to save a lot for our kids' education. But anyone who is smart enough and wants to work hard enough can get a college education. We ended up getting a lot of assistance and the local Masonic Lodge gave Josh a scholarship. He also worked really hard – just as I had done – to help pay his way through the Culinary Institute.

Josh actually did his apprenticeship at the Trapp Family Lodge at the invitation of Executive Chef Michael Martinet. I was very proud of that. I didn't have anything to do with his hiring, either. Josh applied on his own. He did well during his apprenticeship and went on to graduate from the CIA in the upper part of his class.

As youngsters, Josh and Sammy von Trapp were inseparable. Sammy is Johannes von Trapp's son and Maria's grandson. Josh and Sam were the same age and they played in the woods together from the time they could walk. They camped and hiked and hunted and fished and built cabins – all the things boys do in the country.

When Josh went to the CIA, I started to wonder if maybe someday Sammy would take over the Trapp Resort from his dad and Josh would be right there with him running the kitchens.

Today, though Josh is still a superb cook, he is in a new line of work, a plumbing business on Cape Cod. Sammy now heads a ski school in South America. But my hope for another generation at Trapps is still burning brightly.

And I can still dream.

Murbe Haselnuss Stargerl
(Short Dough Hazelnut Bars)

Ingredients:
1 $\frac{1}{3}$ cups flour
$\frac{2}{3}$ cup sugar
5 oz. cold butter
1 egg yolk
2 $\frac{1}{2}$ cups chopped hazelnuts
  (or substitute chopped walnuts)
$\frac{3}{4}$ cup apricot jam
Melted semi-sweet chocolate *(optional)*

Utensils:
Large bowl
Two large, greased
  cookie sheets
Rolling pin and board

Preparation Time: 35 minutes
Oven Temp: 350°F
Baking Time: 8 minutes
Results: 6 bars

Instructions:

1. Mix flour with sugar in a bowl.
2. Separate the egg; save the white aside for step 6.
3. Add egg yolk, butter, and hazel nuts or walnuts to bowl.
4. Work into dough with fingertips and knead quickly into a smooth, firm dough.
5. Cut dough in half, then divide each half into thirds. Roll each piece and fold into tubes about 9 inches long. Transfer tubes to cookie sheet.
6. Brush with egg white.
7. Preheat oven to 350°F. Bake for 8 minutes, then remove from the oven.
8. While tubes are baking, warm the apricot jam. When tubes are removed from oven, spoon the warm jam into the center of the tubes.
9. Cool and cut into bars.
10. For a special treat, bar ends can be dipped in melted chocolate and allowed to cool on a wire rack.

Store Short Dough Hazelnut bars in a tight container or freeze.

Ischeler Krapferln

Ingredients:

2 cups all-purpose flour
1 cup butter
$\frac{1}{2}$ cup granulated sugar
$\frac{3}{4}$ cup ground walnuts
$\frac{1}{4}$ tsp. cinnamon
2 cups melted semi-sweet baker's
    chocolate for coating
$\frac{1}{2}$ cup raspberry preserves for filling
Whole walnuts – one for each pastry

Utensils:

Medium bowl
Small bowl & larger pot
Floured board and rolling pin
Two large, floured and
    buttered or non-stick cookie
    sheets
Small round cookie cutter

Preparation Time: 20 minutes
Oven Temp: 350°F
Baking Time: 8 minutes
Results: 36 rounds or 18 pastries

Instructions:

1. **Place butter, sugar, ground walnuts, flour, and cinnamon in a large bowl and work into a dough.**

2. **Roll out to $\frac{1}{8}$ inch thick and cut circles about $1\frac{1}{2}$ - 2 inches in diameter and place pastry rounds on cookie sheet.**

3. **Preheat oven to 350°F. Bake rounds for 8 minutes.**

4. **Melt enough semi-sweet chocolate in a metal pan placed in water that has recently boiled to make 2 cups. May also be melted in microwave using proper container.**

5. **Cool and sandwich with raspberry preserves. Dip "sandwiches" in melted chocolate and place a walnut on each one. Place back on lightly oiled baking sheet, and cool.**

Store Ischeler Krapferln in a tightly sealed container or freeze.

Lemon Rings

Ingredients:

Cookie Dough
1 cup all-purpose flour
1 tsp. baking powder
1 cup corn starch
8 Tbsp. *(1 stick)* butter
½ cup sugar
5 egg yolks
1 Tbsp. lemon zest

Lemon Glaze
2 cups confectioners sugar
1 tsp. lemon zest
Yellow food coloring
Lemon juice

Topping *(optional)*
1 ½ cups chopped
  pistachios

Utensils:
Medium bowl
Two large, greased
  cookie sheets
Fluted pastry cutter

Preparation Time: 80 minutes
Oven Temp: 350°F
Baking Time: 10 minutes
Results: 24 Lemon Rings

Instructions:

1. Place dry ingredients in a bowl and mix together.
2. Add yolks, lemon zest, and butter. Mix to a smooth dough. Chill for about an hour in the refrigerator.
3. Roll out to ¼ inch thick and cut rings using a fluted pastry cutting wheel.
4. Preheat oven to 350°F. Bake Lemon Rings for 10 minutes until golden brown.
5. While Lemon Rings are cooling, mix glaze by combining the sugar, lemon zest, and one drop of yellow food coloring. Add enough lemon juice to make glaze spreadable.
6. Glaze Lemon Rings with lemon glaze and sprinkle with optional topping of chopped pistachios.

Store Lemon Rings in a tight container or freeze.

A Few Fish Stories

I am a ninth generation Vermonter and I love to hunt and fish. I'd hate to have to make a decision about whether I could hunt or fish.

I learned how to catch big fish from my dad, who was a full-blooded

Abenaki Native American and a meat fisherman. He loved to fish – but for him fishing meant keeping his family fed. So he knew all the tricks for catching big fish. He even made his own lures – something I still do today. For a while, the Faye Record Spoon lure was sold in stores all around New England.

I used to have a route I would take every spring in my International Harvester Scout Travelall. I ripped the back out of the truck so I could sleep in it. Almost as soon as the ice had cleared off the lakes in the spring, my dog Spencer and I would head out for ten days fishing. We would cover all the Northern Vermont lakes until I had a cooler full of fish or until I had caught a fish of record size. Spencer and I would sleep in the same sleeping bag to keep warm. When we got home, Bonnie always said she wasn't sure who needed a bath more – me or the dog.

People don't picture Vermont lakes as having 35 pound fish in them. But some of the lakes and ponds up here have fish in them that are awesome. People just never realize they are there. A lot of our lakes are very cold and very deep. The big fish live deep and only come up in the spring. To catch the big fish, you have to learn how to fish deep and that's what my dad taught me. And sometimes I have pretty good luck.

These days, I am a sport fisherman and I catch and release most fish. But there is nothing I enjoy more than having a big fish on a tight line and watching it jump. I fish all the Northern lakes – Willoughby, Seymour, Caspian, Echo, Big and Little Avril. I spend as much time as I can on the water and I spent so much time at Willoughby that some of my friends started calling me the Mayor of Westmore.

The biggest fish I ever caught in Vermont was a lake trout that was 33 pounds 12 ounces. The record for the state is 34 pounds. If I live long enough, I would like to catch a 35 pounder so that the state record is once again held by a native Vermonter.

Butternut Cookies

Ingredients:

Dough
1 cup butter *(2 sticks)*
1/2 cup granulated sugar
1 egg yoke
1 Tbsp. heavy cream
1 tsp. vanilla
2 cups all-purpose flour
1/2 tsp. baking powder

Coating
(do not mix together)
1/2 cup pecans chopped
1 egg white

Dusting
1/2 tsp. cinnamon
1/2 cup confectioners sugar

Utensils:
Large bowl
Two cookie sheets

Preparation Time: 15 minutes
Oven Temp: 350°F
Baking Time: 15 minutes approximately
Results: 4 dozen cookies

Instructions:

1. Place ingredients for dough in a large bowl and mix well.
2. Scoop or divide dough into 48 pieces. Roll into balls, dip in egg white and then roll in pecans.
3. Place on greased cookie sheets and press slightly.
4. Bake at 350°F for approximately 15 minutes.
5. Cool and dust with cinnamon and confectioners sugar.

Poppy Cheese Sticks

Ingredients:

1 tsp. fresh garlic

1 cup cottage cheese

1 cup butter *(soft, 2 sticks)*

1 ¾ cup all-pupose flour

½ cup Parmesan cheese

1 tsp. paprika *(optional)*

1 Tbsp. poppy seeds

Utensils:
Large bowl
Floured board
Two cookie sheets

Preparation time: 10 minutes
Oven temp: 375°F
Baking time: About 10 minutes until
   golden on edges
Results: 6 dozen

Instructions:

1. Place ingredients in large bowl and mix together.
2. Roll out to ¼ inch thick on floured board.
3. Cut into sticks, or any shape.
4. Bake at 375°F for approximately 10 minutes or until golden on edges.

Mt. Mansfield
Maple Pecan Drop Cookies

Ingredients:

2 cups Vermont maple syrup

2 whole eggs

1 cup *(2 sticks)* melted butter

2 tsp. baking powder

4 cups all-purpose flour

1 cup chopped pecans

Utensils:

Large bowl

Greased cookie sheet

Preparation Time: 15 minutes

Oven Temp: 375°F

Baking Time: 12 minutes

Results: 4 dozen cookies

Instructions:

1. **Place all ingredients into bowl and mix together.**
2. **Scoop or drop cookie glob onto a greased baking sheet.**
3. **Preheat oven to 375°F. Bake cookies for about 12 minutes.**
4. **Cool and serve.**

Store Mt. Mansfield Maple Pecan Drop Cookies in a tight container or freeze.

Othello Cookies

Ingredients:

3 cups all-purpose flour
3 egg yolks
3/4 cup granulated sugar
5 ounces butter *(warmed until soft)*
5 ounces margarine *(warmed until soft)*
2 cups raspberry or apricot preserves
3 cups finely chopped walnuts
3 egg whites

Utensils:

Large bowl
Two large, greased
  cookie sheets

Preparation Time: 15 minutes

Oven Temp: 375°F
Baking Time: 20 minutes then
    10 minutes to glaze preserves
Results: 48 cookies

Instructions:

1. **Allow butter to soften, warming up for about ½ hour to room temperature.**

2. **In a large bowl, combine butter, margarine, granulated sugar, egg yolks, and all-purpose flour. Work ingredients by hand to form a medium stiff dough.**

3. **Roll dough out into 1 inch balls, dip in egg white and roll in chopped walnuts.**

4. **Make an indentation in the middle of each cookie with a finger or a wooden spoon.**

5. **Preheat oven to 375°F. Bake for about 20 minutes, then remove from the oven.**

6. **Pipe or spoon preserves into the indentation.**

7. **Return to the oven for about 10 minutes to glaze the preserves. Cool and serve.**

Store Othellos in a tight container or freeze.

Pecan Snowballs

Ingredients:

3/4 cup confectioner's sugar
1 cup butter *(2 sticks)*
2 cups cake flour
1/2 cup pecans, finely chopped
Vanilla, to taste

Utensils:

Large bowl
Non-stick cookie sheet

Preparation Time: 15 minutes
Oven Temp: 350°F
Baking Time: 10 - 12 minutes
Results: 2 dozen snowballs

Instructions:

1. **Place all ingredients into bowl and mix together.**
2. **Roll into 1 inch balls and place on nonstick cookie sheet.**
3. **Preheat oven to 350°F. Bake Snowballs for 10 - 12minutes.**
4. **Cool and roll in additional confectioner's sugar.**

Store Pecan Snowballs in a tight container or freeze.

My Daughter The Athlete

If Josh took after me by becoming a chef, Tori most definitely took after her mom by being an athlete and sportswoman.

Tori has been an athlete all her life. In high school, she was on champion field hockey, basketball and softball teams. She was one of the first to play women's ice hockey and was a tenacious player. In college, she played sports and led the softball league in stolen bases. And today, she is carrying on her love of sports as the athletic director for the local high school and as the director for the Stowe Recreation Program.

Though she always loved to fish, she never took up hunting. For many years, she went with me in the woods, but only to tag along. Then a boyfriend introduced her to bow hunting and, because it was athletic, she decided to try archery. She practiced hard and her first year out she brought home a nice deer. And since then she has been an avid bow hunter.

This past year, she became the state's number one woman bow shooter in a competition at the local fish and game club.

Now she has taken up black powder musket hunting as well and the two of us go out in the fall. She even convinced me to take up bow hunting, which I now enjoy.

Whether you like outdoor sports or not, there are few things that bind a family together as tightly as the time shared in the woods or at camp. Hunting and fishing are Vermont traditions and like all the values and traditions that we pass on from generation to generation, they have helped make Vermont what it is.

Country Sunshine Crackers

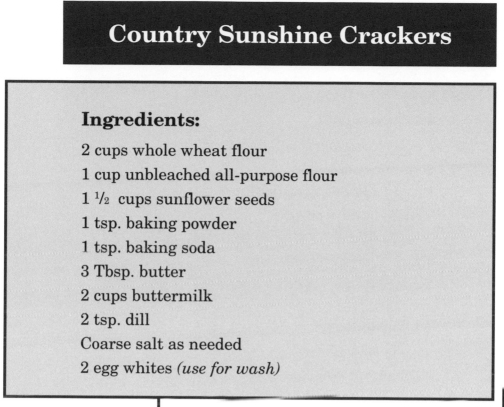

Ingredients:

2 cups whole wheat flour

1 cup unbleached all-purpose flour

1 ½ cups sunflower seeds

1 tsp. baking powder

1 tsp. baking soda

3 Tbsp. butter

2 cups buttermilk

2 tsp. dill

Coarse salt as needed

2 egg whites *(use for wash)*

Utensils:
Large bowl
Three cookie sheets
   lightly greased
Rolling pin

Preparation Time: 10 minutes
Oven Temp: 350°F
Baking Time: 10 minutes approximately
   until crispy
Results: 5 - 6 dozen

Instructions:

1. **Place all dry ingredients in large mixing bowl. Cut in butter.**

2. **Add buttermilk and dill and mix lightly until a dough forms. Allow dough to rest for about 10 minutes.**

3. **Roll the dough out very thin *(about $1/16$ of an inch thick)*, and allow it to rest for about 5 minutes.**

4. **Cut dough into cracker shapes and wash with egg white.**

5. **Place crackers on lightly greased cookie sheets and sprinkle with coarse salt. Prick crackers with a fork.**

6. **Bake at 350°F for 8 - 10 minutes or until crispy.**

Corn and Cheddar Crackers

Ingredients:

2 cups unbleached all-purpose flour

1 ½ cups cornmeal

½ cup whole wheat flour

½ tsp. baking powder

1 tsp. salt

4 tsp. dijon mustard

2 cups sharp cheddar *(shredded)*

2 whole eggs

½ cup olive oil

¾ cup cold water

Kosher salt & 1 eggwhite

Utensils:

Large bowl

Lightly floured board

Rolling pin

Two cookie sheets

Preparation time: 30 minutes

Oven temp: 375°F

Baking time: About 15 minutes or until golden

Results: 3 dozen

Instructions:

1. **Combine all ingredients, except salt and eggwhite, in large bowl and mix to dough.**

2. **Roll out to thickness of pie dough, (*⅛ inch thick*) on a lightly floured board.**

3. **Cut into cracker shapes and place on cookie sheets.**

4. **Brush with eggwhite and sprinkle with salt.**

5. **Bake at 375°F for 15 minutes or until golden.**

Ingredients:

Dough
1 ¼ pounds *(5 sticks)* butter
1 ¼ pounds cream cheese
2 ½ cups sour cream
8 ½ cups all-purpose flour

2 Cups Filling
(suggestions below)
Any pie filling
Peanut butter
Raspberry preserves
Cinnamon and sugar
Apricot preserves
Strawberry preserves

Utensils:
Large bowl
Two greased baking
  sheets
Rolling pin

Preparation Time: 45 minutes
Oven Temp: 375°F
Baking Time: 10 minutes
Results: 48 pieces

Instructions:

1. **Mix butter and cream cheese together, beating until creamy.**
2. **Add sour cream and flour and mix into dough. If too soft to roll out, chill for 20 minutes.**
3. **Divide dough in half and then half again.**
4. **Roll each piece of dough into a rectangle about ⅛-inch thick. Spread filling of your choice on top of dough and roll up. Total filling: 2 cups or ½ cup per rectangle.**
5. **Cut into 1-inch pieces and place on greased baking sheets.**
6. **Preheat oven to 375°F. Bake cookies for about 10 minutes or until lightly browned. Serve warm or cool.**

Store Rugalah in a tightly sealed container or freeze.

Spitsbuben Cookies
(Rascals)

Ingredients:

Dough
2 cups *(4 sticks)* butter or
   margarine *(warmed until soft)*
1 ¼ cups granulated sugar
3 egg yolks
4 ½ cups all-purpose flour
1 tsp. lemon zest
Jar apricot preserves

Lemon Icing
1 ½ cups sifted
   confectioners sugar
4 – 5 Tbsp. lemon juice
1 drop yellow food coloring
½ tsp. lemon zest
1 Tbsp. hot water

Utensils:
Large bowl
Stainless steel or glass
   medium-sized bowl
Floured board and rolling pin
Sifter
Two large, greased cookie sheets
Diamond-shaped cookie cutter

Preparation Time: 25 minutes
Oven Temp: 375°F
Baking Time: About 6 minutes
Results: About 48 cookies

Instructions:

1. **Allow butter to soften, warming up for about ½ hour to room temperature.**
2. **In a large bowl, combine butter, margarine, granulated sugar, egg yolks, lemon zest, and all-purpose flour. Work ingredients by hand to form a workable dough.**
3. **Roll dough out approximately ¼ inch thick. Cut into diamond shapes.**
4. **Preheat oven to 375°F. Bake cookies for about 6 minutes or until slightly golden on the edges. Cool.**
5. **While cooling, make the lemon icing. Put sugar and lemon juice in a stainless steel or glass bowl. Add hot water, lemon zest, and color. Stir into a smooth icing. If too thick, add more water. If too thin, add more confectioners sugar.**
6. **When cookies are cool, spread apricot preserves on half of the cookies and sandwich with the other half. Ice top of each cookie with lemon icing and allow icing to set.**

Store Rascals in a tight container or freeze.

Super Shortbread Cookies

Ingredients:

Shortbreads
2 cups all-purpose flour
$\frac{1}{2}$ cup confectioners sugar
$\frac{1}{2}$ tsp. salt
1 cup margarine
$\frac{1}{4}$ tsp. baking powder

Easy Glaze
$\frac{1}{2}$ cup granulated sugar
$\frac{1}{4}$ cup butter (*$\frac{1}{2}$ stick*)
$\frac{1}{4}$ cup milk
$\frac{3}{4}$ cup confectioners sugar
$\frac{1}{4}$ tsp. salt
Dash vanilla or almond flavor
  color if desired

Utensils:
Large bowl
Two large, non-stick cookie
  sheets
Shaped cookie cutters
Wire mesh cooling rack

Preparation Time: 35 minutes
Oven Temp: 375°F
Baking Time: 10 - 12 minutes
Results: 48 shortbreads

Instructions:

1. Beat the margarine and sugar until it is smooth.

2. Add remaining ingredients and mix into a smooth dough.

3. Roll out on a floured board to $\frac{1}{4}$ inch thick and cut into desired shapes.

4. Preheat oven to 375°F and bake shortbreads for 10 – 12 minutes on a non-stick cookie sheet.

5. While shortbreads are cooling, make glaze by combining $\frac{1}{2}$ cup granulated sugar, $\frac{1}{4}$ cup butter, and $\frac{1}{4}$ cup milk in a small saucepan.

6. Bring to a boil and remove from heat as soon as boiling begins.

7. Add confectioners sugar, salt, and vanilla. Whisk until smooth.

8. When shortbreads are cool, dip in glaze and allow to dry. A wire mesh cooling rack works well.

Store shortbreads in a tight container or freeze.

My Fifteen Minutes

They say that everyone gets to be famous for fifteen minutes. I only got six.

One year we were contacted by one of the major TV home shopping channels which was planning on filming a show from the von Trapp Family Lodge parking lot. It was during fall foliage and they were looking for Vermont products to feature on the segment.

So we agreed to make 2,500 Linzertortes that they could sell on TV.

Now to put that in perspective, on an average day we make between one and two dozen Linzertortes for our guests and visitors,

so this was going to be a major undertaking. Not only did we have to make the Linzertortes, but I had to design a special box so the Linzertortes wouldn't get crushed during shipping and we had to go out and buy a shrink-wrapping machine to seal them all, which we did by hand.

But it was when we realized how much freezer space 2,500 Linzertortes take that we knew we had bitten off more than we expected. We filled the walk-in freezer at the bake shop; we filled the freezers at the lodge; by the time we were done, we had filled every cooler and cold room on the property floor-to-ceiling, front-to-back, with boxes of Linzertortes. Our dining room staff could barely squeeze in the food we needed for our guests at the lodge!

I also got a lesson on the power of television, because on the day of the show, they sold all 2,500 Linzertortes in six minutes! We spent a couple of days addressing packages to the four corners of North America. To this day, we still get calls for mail-order Linzertorte.

And I'm still waiting for my last nine minutes of fame.

Chocolate Pecan Crescents

Ingredients:

Dough
1/8 tsp. cinnamon

1 cup butter *(2 sticks)*

1/4 cup confectioners sugar

1 tsp. vanilla

1/4 tsp. salt

1 Tbsp. water

2 cup all-purpose flour

2 cups ground pecans

Topping
2 cups melted
   tempered chocolate

Colored jimmies

Chocolate stripes

Utensils:
Large bowl

Floured board

Two cookie sheets
   lightly greased

Preparation Time: 20 minutes

Oven Temp: 325°F

Baking Time: 30 minutes approximately
   until golden

Results: 2 dozen

Instructions:

1. **Place all dry ingredients except chocolate in large mixing bowl and mix to a dough.**

2. **Roll out on floured board into 1 inch diameter rolls and cut into 1 inch pieces. Form crescents.**

3. **Place on cookie sheets and bake at 325°F for approximately 30 minutes until golden.**

4. **Cool and dip into melted chocolate.**

5. **Decorate with colored jimmies or chocolate stripes.**

Chocolate Apricot Chews

Ingredients:

Dough

1 ½ cups unbleached all-purpose flour
½ cup unsweetened cocoa powder
½ cup butter *(soft, 1 stick)*
1 cup sugar
¼ tsp. baking soda
¼ tsp. baking powder
2 whole eggs
1 ½ tsp. vanilla extract

Dried Apricots

Cut in quarters as needed

Topping

1 cup semi-sweet
   chocolate chips

½ cup sweetened
   condensed milk

Utensils:

Large bowl
1 oz. scoop
Two cookie sheets
Double boiler

Preparation Time: 25 minutes
Oven Temp: 350°F
Baking Time: 10 - 12 minutes
Results: 4 dozen approximately

Instructions:

1. **Place ingredients for dough in large bowl and mix to a dough.**

2. **Roll dough out into ropes that are 1 inch in diameter and cut into 1 inch sections, or scoop the dough using a 1 ounce scoop. Roll the 1 ounce pieces into balls.**

3. **Place balls on a cookie sheet and press them down slightly. Press your thumb into the center of each cookie to make an indentation in the middle. Place a piece of apricot in the indentations.**

4. **Place ingredients for topping in a double boiler and melt together.**

5. **Bake cookies at 350°F for 10 - 12 minutes. Place a spot of chocolate over each cookie and allow them to cool.**

Topfen Kipferl
(Cheese Croissants)

Ingredients:

1 cup cottage cheese

1 cup *(2 sticks)* butter

2 rounded cups all-purpose flour

2 Tbsp. grated parmesan cheese

4 Tbsp. poppy seeds

Utensils:
Large bowl
Two large, greased
   cookie sheets
Sharp knife

Preparation Time: 15 minutes
Oven Temp: 350°F
Baking Time: 15 minutes
Results: 4 dozen croissants

Instructions:

1. **Mix the ingredients and work together to form a dough.**
2. **Roll dough out into several 1 inch ropes, about 8 inches long. Slice into 1 inch pieces.**
3. **Form into crescent shapes.**
4. **Preheat oven to 350°F and bake for 15 minutes or until lightly golden.**

Store Topfen Kipferl in a tight container or freeze.

Vermont Cheddar Cheese Crackers

Ingredients:

8 oz. sharp or extra sharp Vermont cheddar cheese
8 oz. *(2 sticks)* butter *(warmed until soft)*
1 ³/₄ cup all-purpose flour
Paprika *(if desired)*
Grated parmesan *(if desired)*

Utensils:

Large bowl
Floured board
Lightly greased cookie
   sheet
Cookie cutter

Preparation Time: 15 minutes
Oven Temp: 375°F
Baking Time: 8 - 10 minutes
Results: About 4 dozen crackers,
   depending on size of cutter

Instructions:

1. **Allow butter to soften, warming up for about ¹/₂ hour to room temperature.**
2. **Mix flour, butter, and cheddar cheese into a dough. Add parmesan if desired.**
3. **Roll out ¹/₄ inch thick on floured board and cut with cookie cutter.**
4. **Sprinkle lightly with paprika if desired.**
5. **Preheat oven to 375°F and bake for 8 - 10 minutes or until lightly golden.**
6. **Allow to cool and serve alone or with dip.**

Cranberry Almond Delights

Ingredients:

Dough

3 cups unbleached all-purpose flour

2 cups whole wheat flour

2 cups light brown sugar

2 tsp. baking powder

½ tsp. baking soda

½ tsp. cinnamon

1 ½ cups butter
(solft, 3 sticks)

2 whole eggs

¼ cup orange juice

1 cup dried cranberries

½ cup sliced almonds

Orange Icing

1 cup confectioners sugar

½ tsp. grated orange zest

3 to 4 tsp. orange juice

Utensils:
Large bowl
Cookie sheet
1 oz. scoop

Preparation Time: 15 minutes
Oven Temp: 350°F
Baking Time: 12 - 14 minutes
Results: 2 dozen

Instructions:

1. **Place ingredients for dough in large bowl and mix into a dough.**

2. **Scoop the dough in approximately 1 ounce portions onto a cookie sheet.**

3. **Bake at 350°F for 12 - 14 minutes or until lightly browned.**

4. **Mix orange icing ingredients together.**

5. **While the cookies are still warm, drizzle them with orange icing.**

The Saga Of Big Ben

The bake shop at von Trapps is very much a team effort and I have had a lot of wonderful employees over the years. But the one person who really stands out is Ben Bishop because the two of us are probably the most unlikely looking pair of pastry chefs you could ever find.

I had known Ben since he was a youngster. Ben was the youngest of 14 children. He had spent a lot of time in foster care and had a troubled youth. I actually first hired Ben when I was haying a field next to my house and needed to hire someone with a strong back to toss bales onto the hay wagon. At 6'5" and about 450 pounds, Ben looked big. But none of us realized how strong he really was until he started haying that day.

Ben could pick up two hay bales in one hand – each bale weighs about 100 pounds – and toss them two-at-a-time over his head onto the top of the wagon with enough force to almost knock my neighbor off the top of the wagon.

Though I didn't expect much from him when I first hired him, he showed that he was not only strong, but he had a tremendous work ethic and was really intelligent. So I asked him if he would like to work in the bake shop and learn to be a baker and pastry chef.

Stories about Ben's strength became legendary at the Trapp Family Lodge. One day, a large grounds maintenance tractor sideslipped and got stuck against a fence near the bakery. It couldn't move forward or backwards and the driver asked us to call a tow truck to pull it out. Instead, Ben went outside and literally picked up the front of the tractor and set the front wheels over and went right back to making pastries. On another occasion, a full-size Dodge pickup got a flat in the bake shop parking lot. Ben said he would be glad to lift the back of the truck up onto blocks for the owner. Of course none of us believed he could do it. But he squatted down, put his hands under the bumper, and lifted it up. Another time, someone bet him that he couldn't do a handstand. Not only did he do a handstand, he walked – on his hands – up the driveway.

We ended up working together for nine years and he is one of my best friends and fishing buddies. He even got asked to become a pro-wrestler, but he liked to bake and wanted to be a chef more than anything. He still works in Stowe and is a fine chef and baker. He is also a foster parent himself – committed to giving back to the community.

And I am godfather to his son.

Rum Walnuss Horns

Ingredients:

Murbteig Cookie Dough
1 cup (2 sticks) butter
³/₄ cup sugar
2 egg yolks
2 ¹/₂ cups all-purpose flour
Leftover pie crust pastry
(see page 47)

Filling
5 cups ground walnuts
1 ¹/₂ cups Vermont honey
3 Tbsp. rum
1 whole egg
1 cup bread crumbs

Utensils:
Two medium bowls
Floured board
Two large, greased and
floured cookie sheets

Preparation Time: 40 minutes
Oven Temp: 375°F
Baking Time: 20 minutes
Results: 16 horns

Instructions:

1. Mix the butter, sugar, egg yolks, and flour together into a smooth pastry. Mix with an equal amount of leftover pie crust pastry *(from Island Coconut Custard Pie, page 47)*.

2. Divide in half and then divide each half into eight. Roll out on floured board into ovals about ¹/₈ inch thick. Set aside.

3. Make walnut filling by combining all ingredients and mixing until smooth. Spread filling on each pastry oval and roll into crescent shape.

4. Preheat oven to 375°F. Bake Rum Walnuss Horns for 20 minutes until golden. Cool and serve.

5. For an extra treat, dip ends in melted chocolate and allow to set on a wire rack *(see page 100, steps 4 & 5)*.

Store Walnuss Horns in a tight container or freeze.

Breakfast Treats

Hot Homemade English Muffins

Ingredients:
6 cups all-purpose flour
2 cups warm water *(about 110 degrees)*
2 oz. *(1/2 stick)* butter, melted
2 Tbsp. Saf-instant yeast
¼ cup granulated sugar
¾ Tbsp. salt
1 cup milk powder
2 whole eggs
1 cup yellow corn meal for sprinkling on baking sheet

Utensils:
Large bowl
Floured board
Baking sheet sprinkled with
    cornmeal
Second baking sheet, lightly oiled
Rolling pin
Round 3 ½ inch cookie cutter

Preparation time: 25 minutes
Oven temp: 350°F
Baking time: About 20 minutes or
    until golden
Results: 20 muffins

Instructions:
1. Place milk powder, sugar, and salt into bowl.
2. Add warm water, then add flour, eggs, and butter. Add yeast last.
3. Mix and knead for about 8 minutes into smooth dough. Let rest for 10 minutes.
4. Turn onto a floured board and roll out to ½ inch thick. Let rest again for about 10 minutes. Cut out with round cookie cutter.
5. Place on baking sheet sprinkled with yellow cornmeal. Dust tops with cornmeal and place a second lightly oiled baking sheet on top of the muffins – weighting the top pan if necessary.
6. Preheat oven to 350°F. Bake for about 20 minutes. Serve warm.

Ingredients:

Dough

1 cup warm half and half

¼ pound sweet butter *(1 stick)*

2 large eggs

1 ½ tsp. salt

6 Tbsp. light brown sugar

½ tsp. each lemon and orange zest

4 cups all-purpose flour

2 Tbsp. Saf-instant yeast

Glaze

1 cup confectioners sugar

¼ cup heavy cream

½ tsp. each of lemon and orange zest

Utensils:

Large bowl

Two muffin tins or cookie sheets

Preparation time: 15 minutes

Oven temp: 350°F

Baking time: Approx. 40 minutes or until golden

Results: 1 dozen

Instructions:

1. **Place ingredients in large bowl and mix to straight dough.**
2. **Let rise to ⅔ the size.**
3. **Divide into 12 pieces and place in muffin tins or on cookie sheets.**
4. **Bake at 350°F for approximately 40 minutes or until golden.**
5. **Mix ingredients for glaze together.**
6. **Let cookies cool slightly and glaze.**

Cheddar and Pepper Scones

Ingredients:

3 cups all-purpose flour

$\frac{1}{2}$ tsp. baking soda

3 Tbsp. baking powder

1 Tbsp. sugar

1 cup sharp cheddar cheese shredded

$\frac{1}{4}$ pound butter *(1 stick)*

1 $\frac{3}{4}$ cups buttermilk

2 tsp. coarse black pepper

Egg wash

1 beaten egg

Utensils:

Large bowl
Floured board
Rolling pin
Two cookie sheets
Round 2 $\frac{1}{2}$ inch
    biscuit cutter

Preparation time: 20 minutes

Oven temp: 400°F

Baking time: About 15 - 20 minutes or
    until golden

Results: 2 dozen

Instructions:

1. **Place dry ingredients into large bowl and mix together.**
2. **Add buttermilk and mix to a soft dough.**
3. **Put out onto well floured board and roll to $\frac{3}{4}$ inch thick.**
4. **Cut with 2 $\frac{1}{2}$ inch biscuit cutter and transfer to cookie sheets.** *(Any shape cutter may be used)*
5. **Brush with beaten egg wash.**
6. **Bake at 400°F for 15 –20 minutes until golden. Do not over bake.**

Lowfat Deer Camp Doughnuts

Ingredients:

4 ½ cups all-purpose flour
1 ¾ cups warm water *(about 110 degrees)*
2 tsp. Equal artificial sweetener
1 tsp. nutmeg
⅓ cup canola oil
3 Tbsp. Saf-instant yeast
1 cup powdered skim milk
1 tsp. salt
2 whole eggs
Bakers snow
  *(One cup cornstarch mixed with one cup
  confectioners sugar)*

Utensils:

Large bowl

Floured board

Lightly greased or
  paper lined pan

Doughnut cutter

Preparation time: 15 minutes

Oven temp: 350°F

Baking time: About 20 minutes or
  until lightly golden

Results: 24 donuts

Instructions:

1. Dissolve powdered milk in warm water. Whip in eggs and oil.

2. Add remaining ingredients, except bakers snow, and fold into a wet dough.

3. Roll out ¾ inches thick on a floured board and cut out doughnuts. Place in pan.

4. Allow doughnuts to rise for 30 minutes.

5. Preheat oven to 350°F. Bake donuts for 20 minutes until slightly golden.

6. Cool and dust with bakers snow or cinnamon. Serve with hot coffee.

Prayer Answered
Or Amazing Coincidence

Earlier this year my friend Linda's granddaughter was diagnosed with a rare form of cystic fibrosis. She's a tiny little 6 year old with red hair and an indomitable spirit. Part of the therapy to prolong her life expectancy includes pounding her

on the back and chest at least four times daily and at night, as well, if her breathing is labored.

We visited her in the children's ICU in Burlington after a particularly difficult week. While I'm not an overly religious person, that Tuesday evening, I said a simple prayer, "Lord I wish there is something that I can do to ease her suffering".

The very next day, as I was teaching a baking class for our guests, a pleasant lady asked me if I had any grandchildren. I replied that I had three and my lady friend had four, and that one was extremely ill with C.F. She looked me in the eye and said that she was a respiratory therapy nurse and worked for a medical firm that makes a wonderful new product called the "The Vest", that does the chest P.T. by vibration. In a short time Daelyn had her vest, and was able to travel to Disney Land for her "special wish" from the Make A Wish Foundation and to have lunch with Cinderella.

Personally, I believe my prayer was answered.

St. Timothy's Coffee Cake

Ingredients:

1 cup butter *(2 sticks)*
2 cups sugar
1 Tbsp. vanilla
2 whole eggs
2 cups all-purpose flour
1 tsp. baking powder
$\frac{1}{2}$ tsp. salt
1 tsp. cinnamon
1 cup chopped pecans
$\frac{1}{3}$ cup raisins *(light and dark)* soaked in Grand Marnier
1 cup sour cream
Strong cinnamon sugar *(mix $\frac{1}{2}$ cup granulated sugar with 2 Tbsp. cinnamon)*

Utensils:

Large bowl
Flour sifter
Two tube pans, bundt cake rings or flat cake pans, greased and floured

Preparation time: 25 minutes

Oven temp: 350°F
Baking time: 20 minutes until firm to the touch
Results: 2 large coffee cakes

Instructions:

1. **Mix sugar, butter, and vanilla and beat until creamy. Add eggs and mix well.**

2. **Sift flour, baking powder, salt, and cinnamon into the egg mixture.**

3. **Add pecans, raisins, and sour cream. Mix well.**

4. **Place batter in greased and floured tube pans, bundt cake rings, or flat cake pans.**

5. **Dust with strong cinnamon sugar.**

6. **Preheat oven to 350°F and bake for about 20 minutes until cakes are firm to the touch. Serve warm from the oven.**

Sticky Wheat Breakfast Buns

Ingredients:

Dough
Soft Wheat Dinner Roll Dough
  (See page 37, for complete list of ingredients)
2 cups coarsely chopped pecans
1/2 cup granulated sugar
2 Tbsp. cinnamon
1/2 cup melted butter *(1 stick)*

Glaze
1 cup light brown sugar
1/4 lb. *(1 stick)* butter *(warmed until soft)*

Utensils:
Large bowl
Floured board
Sharp knife
Greased baking sheet

Preparation time: 15 minutes
Oven temp: 350°F
Baking Time: About 20 minues or
   until golden
Results: 24 rolls

Instructions:

1. **Allow butter to soften, warming up for about 1/2 hour to room temperature.**

2. **Mix sugar and cinnamon thoroughly.**

3. **Roll out dough to 1/2 inch thick.**

4. **Brush dough with melted butter; sprinkle evenly with cinnamon sugar and 1 cup of coarsely chopped pecans.**

5. **Roll dough into a log and, using a sharp knife, cut into 1 inch thick slices.**

6. **Preheat oven to 350°F and bake about 20 minutes until golden in color. Serve warm from the oven.**

7. **Form a glaze by mixing warm butter and brown sugar until smooth and creamy. Spread on buns and then sprinkle with remaining pecans.**

Stowe's Finest Maple Oatmeal Muffins

Ingredients:

Batter

2 cups rolled oats
2 cups all-purpose flour
4 Tbsp. baking powder
1 cup Vermont maple syrup
2 Tbsp. maple extract
  *(Optional. Not allowed
  for Vermonters.)*
1 cup milk
$\frac{1}{2}$ tsp. cinnamon
1 cup finely chopped walnuts

Topping

1 cup finely chopped walnuts
1 cup rolled oats
$\frac{1}{4}$ cup granulated sugar

Utensils:

Large bowl
Floured board
Muffin tins for 20
  muffins, lightly
  greased or paper
  lined

Preparation time: 15 minutes

Oven temp: 375°F
Baking time: About 20 minutes or
  until lightly golden
Results: 20 muffins

Instructions:

1. **Place all ingredients into a large bowl and mix until batter is smooth.**

2. **Scoop batter into standard muffin tins, greased or paper lined.**

3. **Mix topping ingredients.**

4. **Sprinkle batter with topping.**

5. **Preheat oven to 375°F and bake for about 20 minutes. Serve warm from the oven.**

Confections

Dark Chocolate Pecan Truffles

Ingredients:

1 cup heavy cream
2 Tbsp. salted butter
6 oz. semi-sweet chocolate, grated
1 cup chopped pecans
1/2 tsp. vanilla
1/4 cup sifted powdered cocoa
2 cups melted semi-sweet baker's
chocolate for coating

Utensils:

Sauce pan
Baking sheet

Preparation time: 30 minutes

Results: About twenty-five 1 inch truffles

Instructions:

1. Place butter and heavy cream in a sauce pan and bring to a boil. Remove from heat as soon as mixture boils and immediately add the 6 oz. grated chocolate, stirring until smooth.

2. Add pecans and vanilla.

3. Chill into a workable dough.

4. Roll chilled dough into 1 inch balls and roll in powdered cocoa, setting truffles on a lightly oiled baking sheet.

5. Chill.

4. Melt enough semi-sweet chocolate in a metal pan placed in water that has recently boiled to make 2 cups. May also be melted in microwave using proper container. Then add remaining powdered cocoa and stir until the mixture thickens.

7. Take chilled balls and dip into melted chocolate to finish. Place back on lightly oiled baking sheet.

8. Refrigerate and serve cool.

Reader's Notes

Reader's Notes